Out of my mind

Out of my mind

Elmer Smith

August Press
Newport News, Va.

OUT OF MY MIND

For information, address August Press,
P.O. Box 6693, Newport News, VA 23606
www.augustpress.net

Illustrations by Signe Wilkinson

Cover photo by
the Philadelphia Daily News staff

Cover design by Rob King

ISBN 0-9635720-6-7

Library of Congress Number   2002112823

First edition

10 9 8 7 6 5 4 3 2 1

To my beloved Mary Ann, who has been at my side for nearly 40 years. I'm not sure why.

And to my mother, Laura Mitchell, who set aside a promising life 55 years ago when the death of her sister left my sister and me in the most-nurturing care God could have provided for us.

It is because they have loved me so lavishly for so long that I feel empowered to come to you in this way.

Also by August Press

Black Journalists: The NABJ Story
Wayne Dawkins, ISBN 0-9635720-4-0

Welcome to Exit 4: Enter at Own Risk
Rosemary Parrillo, ISBN 0-9635720-1-6

Goodnight Sweetheart Goodnight:
The Story of the Spaniels
Richard G. Carter, ISBN 0-9635720-2-4

Sometimes You Get the Bear
Dan Holly, ISBN 0-9635720-5-9

Blackbird
Betty Winston Baye, ISBN 0-9635720-3-2

To order any of these titles
write to P.O. Box 6693
Newport News, VA 23606

Or call (800) 268-4338
Internet: www.augustpress.net

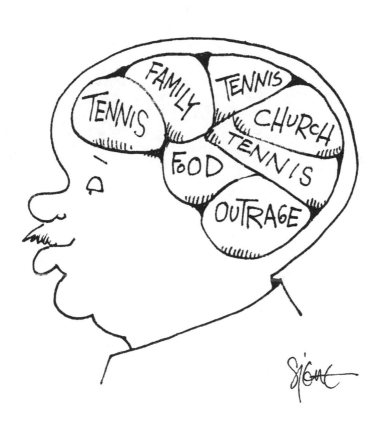

Contents

Chapter 4   **Money Matters**

Chapter 5   **Little Ones**

Chapter 6   **Newsmakers**

Preface

I could barely make out the voice on the other end of the line.

Sounded like a teen-ager calling to comment on the column I had run that day. But there was an urgency in his tone that got my attention.

"Is this Mr. Smith?" he said breathlessly...."I didn't expect to get you.

"But after I read your column in today's paper, I knew I had to try."

The column was about the then-recent death of Hank Gathers, a local legend in Philly playground lore. Gathers' gaudy talents and work ethic had made him an instant star at Loyola-Marymount University by 1992. He was regarded as one of the best big men in the country, an automatic first-round NBA draft choice. But cardiologists had told him his irregular heartbeat could cost him his life if he continued to play basketball. Hank decided that the chance to get his family out of the projects was worth the risk. If he had quit, the life he saved would not have been his own.

He almost made it. He was months away from signing a life-altering NBA contract when his chronic heart condition claimed his life.

The news shook North Philly like one of Hank's rim-rattling slam dunks. Gathers' success had made the schoolboy dream of NBA riches seem accessible to a legion of young gym rats who saw themselves in him. He was the latest in a long line of young players who had parlayed skills sharpened in sweaty struggles on pock-marked playgrounds into prominence and paydays. He left a family, including an infant son, whose future had seemed assured until Hank's sudden death rerouted their destiny.

"I just wanted you to know how much that story meant to me," the kid on the other end of the line was saying. "I was away at basic training and the day I get back to town, here's a story in the paper about my uncle."

I thanked him for taking the time to call (a stock response of mine) and asked him to convey my condolences to the rest of Hank's family.

"No no," he corrected me. "My uncle was Robert Brown."

Robert Brown. I didn't think anyone would remember him. He was a kid I met in the seventh grade at Shoemaker Junior High School. He never made it to the eighth grade. He was killed in an auto accident before his 13th birthday. I had used my memory of him as a lead-in to the Gathers column to make this simple point:

No life is so short, I had said, that it doesn't touch some other life. No one really dies before his time. I just remembered Robert Brown as a kid who loved to laugh and to make everybody around him laugh. I only knew him for a moment, a moment in my life when I needed someone to make me laugh.

But Robert Brown had died many years before the kid on the other end of the line was born.

"I'm sorry," I told him, "This Robert Brown couldn't be your uncle."

"Yes he was," he insisted. "People in my family always talked about him and the way he chuckled, just the way you described it. I've seen pictures of him and I've been hearing about him all my life.

"But he was like a legend. He was never real to me until I read about him in your column. You made my uncle real to me."

The rest of the conversation was a blur. I wished him well, thanked him for the call. But something had changed.

I still sit in a room alone and type words onto a screen. The words are still about what I think or what I feel on any given day.

But I never lose sight of the fact that there are real people out there receiving real messages from those words on the screen. And sometimes the message they receive is different from the one I sent.

It was easier before the kid called. Before that, it was all about me. That's what they tell columnists. It's what I still tell my opinion writing students at Temple University.

Say what you feel and let the chips fall where they may. The minute you become too circumspect, you lose your edge. You go soft.

It's true. Writing columns is not about consensus. If you try to do this job by thrusting a wet finger into the air to see which way the wind is blowing, it will blow right by you. The highest purpose of opinion columns or unsigned editorials is not to make you think what we think. It's simply to make you think. It's a way to engage readers so they are not just passive receptors of the day's events and issues.

Writing columns is not about consensus. If you try to do this job by thrusting a wet finger into the air to see which way the wind is blowing, it will blow right by you. The highest purpose of opinion columns or unsigned editorials is not to make you think what we think. It's simply to make you think. It's a way to engage readers so they are not just passive receptors of the day's events and issues.

The ones who do it best can wade into the most complex morass and emerge with a simple truth. Truth is always simple.

Descartes taught that a truth that is not as understandable to an ignorant peasant as it is to a learned scholar is not truth at all.

My favorite columnists are people like the late Mike Royko who reduced the reality of Chicago to its simplest terms.

Herb Caen's feel for San Francisco made him a household name in that town.

Steve Lopez, a transplanted Philadelphian, wrote about his adopted town with a familiarity that made us natives nod. You read one of their columns and it sounds like something you could have written yourself.

page XIII

Columns don't work because we agree with them. They work because we can relate to them, whether we agree or not.

It's not easy to be mindful of an audience without falling into the trap of trying to adopt their point of view. But that is precisely the thin line where a columnist must find his balance.

For the past 14 years, I've been trying to find that delicate balance. I started writing columns in the sports section of the *Philadelphia Daily News*, became an editorial columnist and a metro columnist. I've tried to be a part of the conversations people are having over dinner or drinks.

The collected musings compiled in this book are a sampling of what has come out of my mind since the first time an editor told me take this space and do what I wanted with it.

Hope it makes you laugh or maybe rekindles a pleasant memory. It may make you angry or even sad. Or maybe I'll get lucky again and you'll find something that means more when you read it than it did when I wrote it.

– Elmer Smith
June 2002

Chapter 1

A Jacksonville, Fla. cop and the plane from which Elmer
Smith's daughter and her boyfriend emerged unscathed (AP)

About me and mine

No point in dad hitting the roof,
Since kids already landed on it

Cheryl's voice was first on the line. So I should have sensed that something was very wrong.

Usually, when my only child and sole heir to the family fortune calls long distance, the operator speaks first.

But this wasn't even a collect call. Something had to be wrong.

"Dad?" she said in her best ice-cool monotone. "I was in a plane crash this morning.

"But don't worry, Aric landed the plane on top of a house and nobody got hurt."

Try putting those thoughts together:

(A) Plane crash.

(B) Landed on house.

(C) Nobody got hurt.

If "A" or "B" is true, then "C" is unlikely. If "A" and "B" are true, then "C" is impossible.

I'm processing all of this when the slightly-less-cool voice of Aric Arnold breaks through. Aric is Cheryl's boyfriend.

"Mr. Smith, sir," he says. "I'm really sorry about this."

And I know he is. But "I'm really sorry about this" sounds like what you tell a girl's father when you accidentally keep her out past curfew.

Seems like there ought to be another sentence for situations where you plummet 1,500 feet to the ground, bounce high enough for a wind gust to lift you back into the air and finally set the plane down on someone's roof.

page 3

I'm not sure what one should say in that situation. I just know the whole conversation is sounding just a bit too cool for me.

I glance across the room at my wife Mary Ann who, by now, is holding an extension phone.

She seems calm, enough. But then, again, she has been a teacher and assistant principal in Philadelphia schools for 23 years. Bouncing Cessnas are the only thing she hadn't dealt with before.

"I did everything I could, sir," Aric is saying. "But the engine just cut out and I couldn't get it started again."

Then Aric tells us a story so incredible, I'm still having trouble believing it. But nobody makes up a story like this.

This all happened Thanksgiving morning just outside Jacksonville, Fla., where Aric lives with his father. He is an aviation operations student at Jacksonville University.

Aric and Cheryl, both 23, have been dating for four years. Mostly, they've been making phone calls and writing letters for the two years since Aric went South to pursue a career as a pilot.

But, somehow, the relationship has progressed to the point where Cheryl wanted to go south to meet Aric's dad and stepmother.

She did say that she and Aric might borrow a plane and take a little spin around town. But that didn't bother me.

Aric seems as settled and level-headed as any young man I know. He has logged well over 300 hours of air time, including almost 200 as the solo pilot of single-engine aircraft like the four-seater he and Cheryl took out.

And, apparently, Aric is an even better pilot than I thought. "We had been flying for about 45 minutes at 3,000 feet," he said. "We were headed in. I was about five miles out. The traffic pattern for the airport is 1,000 feet. So I was at about 1,500 feet and descending gradually.

"The engine just cut out. I tried everything.

"I drew heat off the engine into the carburetor just in case it had iced up. I switched gas tanks in case there was some impurity in the gas.

"I varied the air and gas mixture into the carburetor" – using some type of choke mechanism.

"I did every re-start procedure in the books. But it wouldn't catch."

page 4

Meanwhile, the ground is coming up to meet them at an alarming rate.

The possibility of a hard landing is looming large.

So, I'm thinking, Cheryl must be going nuts about now.

"No, sir," Aric tells me. "She never screamed. Cheryl never panicked."

Now, I know that Cheryl is cool at all costs. It's always been my biggest gripe with her.

I remember taking her out into the back yard before we drove her off to her first year in college. I told her college was something to get excited about.

"Listen, kid," I said, "You're living your life at the wrong temperature. "Stop being so ---- cool."

But if there was ever anything that could break her calm, it was small planes.

"Mr. Smith, sir," he says. "I'm really sorry about this." And I know he is. But "I'm really sorry about this" sounds like what you tell a girl's father when you accidentally keep her out past curfew.

Seems like there ought to be another sentence for situations where you plummet 1,500 feet to the ground, bounce high enough for a wind gust to lift you back into the air and finally set the plane down on someone's roof.

She got so scared flying from Las Vegas to the Grand Canyon on one of those puddle hoppers, she threw up. My wife had to drag her on the plane when it was time to head back to Vegas.

Now, they're trying to tell me that she just eased back and chilled as her life hung in the balance between air and Earth.

I'm a thousand miles away an hour later, and my life flashed before my eyes just listening to this.

"For some reason," she said, "I never panicked.

"I could see Aric was doing all he could."

page 5

Anyway, it all ended well. Aric eased it to the ground but the tail wind was too high for it to actually land. Had something to do with what he called ground effects. But don't ask me.

All I know is that when they got back up into the air, Aric banked it and, somehow, set it down on the roof of 1833 Live Oak Drive.

A guy who lived in the housing development across the road (remind me to send him a Christmas card) put a ladder up to the roof and helped them down.

Cheryl told reporters that she was more frightened climbing down the ladder than she was in the plane.

The owners of 1833 Live Oak drive were out when Aric and Cheryl dropped in. But Lloyd Brown was next door cooking.

"I was amazed," Brown told the Jacksonville *Times Union*. "You just don't see planes sitting on the roofs of houses too often."

Actually, I've seen it at least once too often.

– November 30, 1993

page 6

Slim chance for father of the bride

I told Sherri that I'll be wearing a tuxedo two sizes smaller than my present size when I give my daughter away this spring.

"Won't she be embarrassed?" Sherri asked with a straight face.

I let that pass. That's how I handle all disparaging comments about my present and intended weight. I don't expect people like Sherri to understand. She's as slim and supple as a willow switch.

Besides, we were having this conversation in the cafeteria where I had just piled my plate with enough calories to fuel the Normandy invasion force.

I don't have an eating disorder. People who can't find their mouths with a fork have an eating disorder. I have a love of food. There's a difference.

Thing is, I can take the weight off any time I want to. In fact, I've lost more than 160 pounds in the last 10 years. And even though I'm 15-20 pounds heavier now than I was 10 years ago, it's still a remarkable accomplishment.

So I know I can lose a piddling 20-25 pounds between now and June if I really want to. And I really want to.

It's important, not just as an ego thing. I wouldn't be doing this just for me. It's for my child.

page 7

She can remember the 5-foot-10-inch 180-pounder I was when she was a little girl. So nobody has to tell her that there's a slimmer version of me trapped within this expanding package.

But I'd hate it if she took a look at her slim fiance and a look at her portly dad and started to envision a future with a fat man. I'd have only myself to blame if she broke out running back up the aisle or if she blurted out her ``I do" when the minister asked if anyone knows any reason why these people shouldn't be joined in holy matrimony.

Besides, weight loss is almost too easy nowadays. They've got some stuff now that practically peels it off. Procter & Gamble devoted about $100 million of its research and development budget to a form of fake fat that is already turning up in such staples as low-fat Tastykakes.

So far, the only known side effect is that it upsets some people's guts, which is actually a side benefit for us serious dieters.

But as those of us who have experienced weight loss can tell you, it's not just about diet. It takes a carefully coordinated regimen of diet and exercise to achieve significant weight loss.

Here again, modern technology has transformed this once formidable protocol into something as simple as selecting the right thigh-tightening, tummy-crunching, butt-crunching machinery.

My daughter and I counted six different infomercials for fold-away exercise equipment Saturday morning. I noticed because she was counting out loud. But I let that pass.

They had portable treadmills and cross-country ski simulators. And they had this plunger thing that you hold against your navel and then pull in on to work your abdominal muscles.

Doesn't work for skinny people. You've got to have a navel as deep as a shot glass to anchor this thing.

There was this one infomercial for a machine that worked your leg back and forth like a metronome. It promised to tighten your inner thighs, buttocks and calves while keeping time for junior's piano lesson.

page 8

My personal favorite was for the one where you lie inside these two wheels which then rotate your torso up and back in a kind of semi-automatic sit-up. The guy demonstrating it had an abdomen that looked like an aerial view of a rolling surf at high tide.

So it's not the challenge it used to be, despite the discouraging words offered up recently by a pop psychologist named David Garner. Garner's theory is that everybody's body has a blueprint and you can't build a skyscraper from the plans for a quonset hut.

Garner is chairman of the psychology section of the National Academy for Eating Disorders, which must be the scene of some of the most disgusting research ever conducted. He's been studying eating disorders for 20 years.

Took him 20 years to come up with a theory that could put the National Academy out of business if anybody listened to him. They ought to yank his research grant.

Essentially, what he's saying is that the body has an internal regulator that works to keep its weight in balance. When you start losing weight, Garner claims, the body figures out how to store the same amount of fat with less intake.

Garner's research is being closely followed by the federal government, which is hoping to find a similar internal regulator that can do the same thing with tax dollars. He's still years away from identifying his weight regulator. But that may be close enough for government work.

Thing is that there was a time when I would have hung my heavy frame on his every word. I used to scan the literature for research that proved a milkshake is an important dietary aid.

Where was Dr. David Garner when I was seeking solace? How come he's not working with that team of researchers who are looking for ways to trick the ``fat gene" into producing slim offspring from obese parents?

I hear these guys are about to release findings from an experiment where they mated two hippos who produced a baby built like a greyhound.

– *February 7, 1996*

page 9

Gathering momentum and not looking back

In 1968, the United States Army returned the unused portion of my life. They had barely touched it.

Three years of what the guys in my unit laughingly called military service had left me remarkably unaltered. but on July 5, they turned me out with a check for $600 and the right to say that I answered when my country called.

Course, I didn't tell them that I answered a Bell System 4A switchboard or that my farthest forward advance was 6,000 miles from North Vietnam, or that I spent the war years as a telephone operator at a Nike missile site in Edgmont, Delaware County.

War is hell, even on the West Chester Pike.

The fighting men of C Battery, 3rd Missile Battalion, 43rd Artillery were more likely to earn a Good Housekeeping seal than a Purple Heart. We dodged the draft by joining the Army.

We were manning a site where the standard weapon was a five-ton missile with a nuclear warhead and a maximum range of 100 miles. By the time the war got bad enough to use one of those, our mothers would be engaging the Viet Cong in hand-to-hand combat on the city streets.

There were a few dicey moments. but the men of C Battery somehow managed to keep Delaware County safe for democracy.

page 10

Aside from bullet avoidance, the main benefit of being close to home was that it eased my transition from "military" to civilian life. And that was a tougher transition than you may imagine.

Because by 1968, America and I had outgrown almost every attitude we had comfortably held for much of the "60s. We got out of uniform together.

Our growth rate was phenomenal but hardly painless. Seemed like everybody I knew suddenly stopped believing good would triumph over evil. we weren't even sure which was which.

It was the year that the murder of Bobby Kennedy closed Camelot for good and forced a rude return to reality. Whatever hope we had invested in the Kennedy boys would never pay dividends now.

That year the assassination of Martin Luther King Jr. forced foot soldiers in the civil-rights movement to come to grips with the fact that they could no longer expect America to adjust its racial attitudes just because they had shown her the error of her ways.

I became a black man that year, and took myself and my people more seriously than I ever had before. I read Eldridge Cleaver's "Soul on Ice" and soaked up all the black literature and poetry I could.

I watched Tommie Smith and John Carlos mount a silent protest at the Olympic games and felt proud and powerful. I had only been a lukewarm fan of Cassius Clay because he talked too much and took the title from Sonny Liston, a fighter who hung out in my West Philadelphia neighborhood.

But I loved Muhammad Ali because he showed more guts outside the ring than anybody I had ever seen in it. When he ran his mouth, he pumped my heart.

People like the late Cecil B. Moore, whose profanity and arrogance had turned me off when I was a boy, lit my my fire when I was a man. When he led the marches that ended with the admittance in 1968 of the first black student at Girard College, I stopped asking and started demanding.

But mainly 1968 was the year I started demanding more of myself. Aimlessness was no longer a virtue; a life of lateral moves was comfort I could no longer afford.

I wasn't sure where I was going when the Army gave me back the reins. But I knew it was somewhere straight ahead.

So on July 5, they handed me an honorable discharge and a check for $600. I gave the money to a jeweler on Sansom Street that afternoon and slipped the engagement ring on my girlfriend's finger a few hours later.

We set a December date and started shopping for furniture.

By the end of the week, I was working from 2 a.m. to 9:30 a.m. as a security guard at Strawbridge & Clothier. I probably could have gotten a better job. But I wasn't willing to wait.

That September, I went back to high school full time in the day while I held my night job. It cost me $2,000 but it was the only way I could complete the course I needed to get into college.

A year later, I was a Temple freshman, going to school full time during the day while holding on to my night job.

My wife, by then a Temple senior, and I were expecting our first child.

I was still racing like the devil was in hot pursuit. I rolled for the next few years off the momentum I gathered in 1968.

Maybe that's why I don't remember much of what happened to America that year. It's all a blur.

I do remember that Martin died in April and Bobby Kennedy died in June. I remember feeling that something important had ended.

But then it was July. Time to grow up and take charge of my life.

I haven't spent much time looking back since then.

– *May 30, 1993*

This column was part of a package of columns, stories and pictures commemorating the 25th anniversary of what Philadelphia Daily News editors felt was the most transforming year in modern American history.

page 12

What would we have done in his combat boots?

When we met in 1965, Oliver S. Parker had just returned from Vietnam where he had earned a Bronze Star medal.

I never knew about the Bronze Star until this week, when I read his obituary in the Philadelphia Tribune. In all of our conversations, mostly about the military, he'd never breathed a word to me about his combat experience.

They don't give Bronze Stars to the colonel's driver or the guys who attach toe tags to the corpses they shipped home.

You've got to get close enough to get the war on you. In you.

He kept it in him.

We weren't friends in '65. I was a grunt; Capt. Parker was my commanding officer.

When I ran into him 10 years ago, he was a retired lieutenant colonel, working as a personnel manager at the state office building a block from my desk here.

We'd talk about how he worked his way up from private to master sergeant, before entering Officer Candidate School. He talked about serving in Korea with the 24th Infantry, one of the Buffalo Soldier units of black soldiers who fought Indians on the Great Plains 100 years earlier.

But he didn't talk about combat.

I wonder about guys like that. In '65, I met lots of guys just back from the war.

page 13

Some talked about it expansively and in disgustingly graphic detail.

Others wouldn't talk about it on a dare.

One guy I asked what it was like said: "You ever been scared or lonely? It was like that. Every day."

Thank God, I don't know what that's like or what it's like to trudge through a rice paddy that might be a minefield or to scan a treeline looking for snipers.

I don't know how I'd react in a situation where the cute little kid planting rice next to his mother today might plant a bomb in my backpack tomorrow.

Thank God, I don't know what that's like or what it's like to trudge through a rice paddy that might be a minefield or to scan a treeline looking for snipers. I don't know how I'd react in a situation where the cute little kid planting rice next to his mother today might plant a bomb in my backpack tomorrow.

So I can't know what might prompt a decent man like Bob Kerrey to order the systematic slaying of 20 Vietnamese women and children.

Except that the officer who led his men through that steamy jungle 30 years ago was not a man like Bob Kerrey or the gentle man I knew as Oliver S. Parker.

Men like that don't fight wars. They have to become something very different to survive a war, something some may choose not to remember.

Bob Kerrey's memory of that encounter differs from the chilling tale retold in the New York Times Magazine Sunday by a man who was in his command that day. We know women and children died. But we don't know why.

Whether Kerrey earned his combat medals honorably may be debated. But he has certainly served with distinction since Vietnam.

page 14

He was a moderately successful businessman before becoming a governor and U.S. senator and currently, a university president.

Now, 32 years after the incident, he finds himself arraigned before the people's tribunal for something he may or not have done in our defense.

I don't blame the man who told his version to the Times. It's his life, too. He has his own demons to exorcise.

And I'm not so sure that if I knew all of the details, I'd condone what Kerrey did. But I'm not comfortable judging this Bob Kerrey today for what that Bob Kerrey may have done in 1969 – or what you or I may have done if we had been there.

Oliver S. Parker's last battle ended the way all of ours will.

"He fought hard," his wife Harriet Parker told me. "In the hospital, they called him an old war horse."

Viewing is today at Mount Zion Baptist Church, 50th Street and Woodland Avenue.

Then they will open the ground at Arlington National Cemetery and bury him with his unspoken memories, beside thousands of other silent soldiers.

– May 2, 2001

Attack on America
–The winds of war

Cheryl and Aric have put the house plans on hold for now. War changes things.

They had been looking around the Fayetteville, N.C., area for the right lot and a builder they could trust to build what was to be their first home together.

Except they may not be together.

He is a captain in an Army aviation unit supporting the 82d Airborne Division in Fort Bragg, N.C. Nobody knows for sure where the 82d will be collecting its mail in the next few weeks.

They're not whining. I won't either. This is the life they chose and they know how to deal with it.

It's just that all this war talk has a different resonance for families like theirs.

For the rest of us, "sacrifice" may be as simple as enduring longer lines at airport check-in counters or the rippling effects of a temporarily shaky economy.

The President is right. For our sanity almost as much as for our safety, we need to "hunt down and punish" the perpetrators.

But we need to know that we cannot make them pay a price without paying a price ourselves.

So it just made sense for Cheryl and Aric to hold off on any long-term plans until things stabilize again.

Seems it always makes sense to hold off on any long term plans when you are a military family. Cheryl, who is my daughter, and Aric, her husband, have been bounced from one short-term life to another since they were married five years ago.

page 16

He spent the first year of their marriage in Korea. It was a bad break. But these things happen.

They did get to spend two years together in Savannah, Ga., when he was stationed there. Well, sort of.

He spent four of those months in Nicaragua on disaster duty after floods ravaged that region. And then there were training missions in three different Army posts that kept him away for weeks at a time.

Then he got orders for Fort Lee, Va. They actually shipped their furniture.

But he was only there for a few weeks at a time before he was sent to Alabama for several months of additional training.

Cheryl and the kids never moved to Virginia, opting to move back home until things got settled. But when he got orders to Fort Bragg, it looked like they would be together there for two years.

They were in limbo for a few long weeks while he waited to find out if he was going to be "deployed" to Kosovo with his unit. But he didn't have to go.

So as soon as the school year ended, Cheryl and my granddaughters, Ashley, 12, and Aaliyah, 3, headed gleefully south to be together.

Aric had already gotten approved for a home loan. He enrolled Ashley in her fourth school in her fourth home state. They started searching for lots the day Cheryl got to town.

But everything changed Tuesday. Hijacked airliners crashed into the World Trade Center and the Pentagon.

Some unknown enemy shattered the symbols of American capitalism and military might. And our false sense of security.

So, it just makes sense to put things on hold for right now.

"We're all fine," Cheryl told me when I called Tuesday night.

"Aric's in lockdown," she joked. "We're not sure when he'll be home. But everything else is great."

Maybe this is war. But it's not war as we've known it.

There is no duration, there is no frontline. Even the enemy can change from moment to moment.

page 17

This war against terrorism may be the longest and costliest in American history.

It's gratifying to see our allies step to the fore so soon after one of the darkest moments in our history. Because we can't win this one alone.

But if we fail through diplomacy or intimidation to persuade the people harboring them to turn the perpetrators over to us, we'll be ready to go in and get them.

It may mean ground troops, and digging in on foreign soil for a long time.

It could mean body bags and toe tags and long separations and changed plans and long waits for our boys and girls to get home just long enough to pack up and head out again.

They can handle it. But when the war talk heats up, it's a good idea to know what we're talking about.

– September 14, 2001

Nightmare offers food for thought

I sat straight up in bed, chest heaving, sweat rolling in rivulets down the side of my face. Felt like I had just finished some vigorous exercise.

My wife, still in a tight fetal curl, slept the sleep of the innocent beside me. (So much for the exercise theory).

Besides, I recognized that metallic taste on the tip of my tongue as the flavor of fear. Something had startled me. But what?

Turns out it was just a nightmare, the worst one I ever had involving a portion of food.

Actually, most of my worst dreams involve food. I tend to eat my biggest meals late at night. This gives me nightmares which, in turn, cause me to wake me up in cold sweats.

And since I'm up anyway, I usually head downstairs for a quick snack.

So I've learned to live with an alternating current of snacks and nightmares and snacks and . . .

But this was different. This bad dream wasn't induced by food – it was about food.

You really only remember the last scene in a nightmare. But I can't forget this ending. It may have changed my way of life.

page 19

I remember waking up on an operating table during major surgery. I look up to see a team of surgeons huddled around a cheesesteak, shaking their heads slowly.

Usually, I don't bother guys when they're working. But I figured since they were working on me, maybe I'd better check.

"You guys taking a lunch break?" I asked innocently.

"Nah," the chief surgeon told me. "We just dug this sandwich out of one of your coronary arteries.

"So, we're gonna give you a choice.

"Either you change your eating habits or we can strap you down, cut you open and do one of these cheesesteakectomies every couple years or so."

That one didn't take much deliberating.

I never choose anything that starts with me getting strapped down and cut open.

At least I never consciously choose that.

But, as the doctor was explaining to me, inside-the-chest surgery is a natural by-product of my favorite menu choices.

See, I like hot, buttered anything.

If you smear enough butter on it, I'll eat filet of sole with the shoe still attached.

Like so many of the things I prefer in life, this is bad for me. I know that instinctively.

But nothing drives the point home like the prospect of being surrounded by masked men in lab coats wielding sharp tools.

So this dream is already starting to have a profound effect on my eating habits.

My new mealtime mantra is, "I'll have the salad, hold the dressing." I haven't started craving cottage cheese yet, but I'm definitely a changed man since "the dream."

Actually it wasn't just the dream. I also got a wake-up call from my cardiologist last week.

"Just looked over your thalium stress test," he said. " . . . I think we'd better get you in here for some additional testing."

That wasn't all he said. There was something about arterial flow and other stuff.

page 20

But to tell you the truth, I didn't hear too much after the sentence, "I think we'd better get you in here for some additional testing."

He's going to explain all of it to me tomorrow. In fact he had started to explain it last week.

But when he got to the part about how he was going to insert a tiny TV camera next to my heart through an artery in my groin, I thought maybe I had heard enough for one day.

Somehow, I failed to get that point across to several of my friends and co-workers who have had this proceedure done and love to describe it in detail.

"It's a breeze," this one guy told me.

"The doctor explains everything. You can even watch the whole thing on the television while he's doing it."

I may even order a few wallet-sized snapshots of the inner me. But right now, I don't think so.

My friend Ike called with more than enough information, too.

"Nothing to it," Ike said. "Except that part where they put those two big bricks on your thighs to hold you down."

I thanked him and asked for his cardiologist's name, just to make sure I didn't accidentally end up in the same office.

But other than that, I haven't really taken any extra precautions. An average cardiologist does a dozen of these cardiac catheterizations a week.

I'll probably sit up and let him point out the highlights of my blood flow. I can always lie back down if I see something that looks like a ham sandwich moving along inside my femoral artery.

The important thing is that I'm already well on the way to making the kinds of changes that should keep my circulatory system off television.

I'm eating more sensibly. I haven't had a candy bar or a late-night snack since "the dream." I lost two pounds last week.

And that's not even counting what I sweated off that night I woke up suddenly.

And for the first time in my writing career, I'm starting to work a book.

I've already got a title for it.

I'm calling it "Low Stress and Watercress: A Recipe for a Long but Boring Life."

— October 12, 1993

A reminder: Growing old's not for sissies

I'm standing in the fast food restaurant at 58th and Baltimore when I overhear two young guys grousing about the service.

A lady who had placed her order after theirs had been served before them.

That was all the one kid could take.

"Ay, that ain't right," the one said. "She came in after us."

"Yeah," the other one said. in disgust "They'll probably serve OLD HEAD before they serve us."

Old Head?

I didn't want to believe they were talking about me. But there was no one there except them, the lady who was on her way out with her steaming bag in her hand. And me, Old Head.

I suffered this indignity without reply. But my special sauce was not so special that night.

Later a friend reminded me that Old Head was a term of respect in the parlance of street gangs. The Old Head was at the top of a hierarchy that included "young boys" and "Peewees."

"Yeah," I thought, "the young boys were just giving me my props."

Which worked until about a month later, when I was headed out the back door of our building to the parking lot. A guy in sagging jeans and huge sweatshirt held his wrist up.

"Ay, Old Head" he said, pointing to his wrist. "What time you got."

Not much to hear you tell it, I said. but I said that to myself. To him, I gave the correct time.

I tried to shrug it off. I thought about what my friend had said.

But, I don't know, seems like things sit with you a little longer when you get to be an Old Head.

Then I picked up yesterday's paper and read where the Social Security Administration is beginning to raise the age for retirement with full Social Security benefits. Starting next month the retirement age will increase gradually until people born after 1960 will not be able to collect full benefits until they are 67. At least.

"Revenge of the Old Heads!" I thought. Now the young boys and peewees will pay a price for being born so late.

Then I read the fine print.

Turns out that those of us who had thoughts of retiring early at age 62 (just eight years hence for this Old Head) may want to rethink that option. Because the first casualty of the Social Security rules change is us.

In fact people born in 1938 who will be 62 next year and planned an early retirement will find that the amount of their long-anticipated retirement check will be reduced by almost a percentage point below what they would have gotten if they had been born a year earlier.

And it gets worse. Those of us born between 1943 and 1954 who decide to stick it out until normal retirement age, will find the finish line moved back one year.

We'll have to be 66 to retire with full benefits. And if we want to go out early, we'll suffer a 25 percent reduction in benefits, compared to the 20 percent cut people experience now if they go out at 62 instead of 65.

After that, it gets really complicated. You'd need a calculator and an actuarial table to figure it out with any precision.

But basically, the retirement age will start to climb again at the rate of two months a year. And those who retire early will incur a 30 percent benefit reduction.

page 23

They do sweeten the pot for those of us who decide to work on past our 60s. We'll get a premium of an additional 8 percent if we retire at age 70 compared to the 6 percent premium you get for hanging on to 70 now.

Naturally, they couch these changes in complimentary terms. We can work longer because we're healthier longer than those who came before us, the Social Security Administration claims.

Many of us will retire with our own teeth and still be able to walk almost upright. Of course all those senior citizen discounts that our fathers and mothers enjoyed will be gone because, by then, half the people in America will be our age or older.

And the streets won't be safe for us because the young boys and peewees will be mad as hell because their retirement age will have been raised to 86 by then.

Which may make us Old Heads the last generation of Americans who won't be expected to literally work our way to the grave.

– December 1, 1999

Chapter 2

Passing through

Thanks Bob

Call it neighborhood natural selection or maybe survival of the *fistest*. But by some Darwinian culling of the herd, the sub-species we called tough guys began to emerge by about the fourth grade.

They had thicker necks, flaring nostrils and eyes that narrowed to slits at the least provocation. Some of them had an extra knuckle on each fist. At least that's the way it felt.

I was not one of these. I was of the pencil-necked geek sub-species. We emerged from a gene pool that had only a shallow end. That adrenaline-fueled fight-or-flight reaction which had preserved our primal predecessors was only partially developed in us. We had perfected flight. But our fight trait was recessive.

Territorial imperatives didn't seem all that imperative to us. We were far too evolved to fight over territory or lunch money or just because some tough guy decided to cave in our chest cavities for laughs. The tough guys could reduce themselves to bestial levels if they so chose. We would not respond in kind.

But some kind of response seemed warranted. One afternoon while I was waiting for my chest to reinflate I hit upon a plan that would sustain me through the tough guy years and even into adulthood: I would make them laugh.

I developed a reputation in my West Philly neighborhood for playing the dozens. I could talk about your mama so bad it would make you laugh. Got so good at it that I decided to try it out on one of the thick-necked, slit-eyed, six-knuckled bruisers in the lunchroom. This was a particularly malevolent example of the sub-species whose name I will withhold for fear someone may read this to him. We'll call him Bob.

"Hey Bob," I called to him in across a crowded lunchroom.

"I stopped by to see if you wanted to walk to school with me this morning. "

"Ugh??!!"

"But when I rang the bell, your mother ran from under the porch and bit me on the leg."

What followed was a frightening interval. Highlights of my entire 13-year life flashed before my eyes. Could it all end here, I thought? Would cafeteria workers in hair nets and sensible shoes find small pieces of my broken body between the shepherd's pie and the Beefaroni?

When I came to myself, people were doubled over with laughter. Even Bob. His features softened from the fixed scowl to a kind of tough-guy half-smile.

"That was a good one," Bob said uttering one of the simple sentences he had recently mastered.

It was a moment that set the course for the rest of my life. I found I could say almost anything if it was funny enough. There is no man so mirthless that he can't be made to laugh, no subject so serious that it can not be treated with humor.

That includes a potentially fatal small plane crash when my daughter and her boyfriend crash-landed on the roof of a house on Thanksgiving day, or a four-hour angioplasty to unclog my left anterior descending artery (whatever that is).

Sure, anybody can see the humor in a blocked coronary artery or a near-fatal plane crash. But mass murder, war, famine and pestilence (whatever that is) are all funny when you think about it.

And that's the key. We want you to think about it. The columnist's peculiar conceit is the belief that what we have to say is worth the four minutes and 47 seconds it takes to read a column. But it doesn't much matter what our point is if nobody is still awake when we get to it.

That's why guys like the late Mike Royko or Art Buchwald rarely wrote anything that wasn't funny. For four minutes and 47 seconds of your time, a dozen columnists in huge shoes with flashing, red noses would drive up to your house and pile out of a Volkswagen beetle. We are without shame in this regard.

But it's not just us. What social scientist or theologian can observe the human condition for a full four minutes and 47 seconds without doubling over in laughter. We are a silly species caught in absurd situations.

When precision-equipped Navy frog men in rubber wet suits emerge from the ocean onto Somalian beaches and run into news photographers in flip flops and garish Hawaiian shirts, you've got to laugh.

How can you not laugh? There was nothing funny about the 9-11 tragedy. But half the stuff that happened right after it was hilarious. You're gonna tell me the fact that George Bush was the first President who couldn't get a direct flight to Washington wasn't funny? How about the government-sanctioned sibling rivalry between the FBI and the CIA or former Pennsylvania Governor Tom Ridge color-coding our national security efforts?

When precision-equipped Navy frog men in rubber wet suits emerge from the ocean onto Somalian beaches and run into news photographers in flip flops and garish Hawaiian shirts, you've got to laugh.

You've got to laugh when the Republican Party that has seen the American people reject three of its last four presidents pushes for term limits or when Al Gore begins his run for President by distancing himself from the most popular figure in his party's recent history.

If a guy named Newt who has never had a wife he wouldn't cheat on raises his finger in moral indignation at Bill Clinton's infidelities, you laugh.

Our Bill gave us years of unrelieved yuks. When I see him, I don't know whether to hum "Hail to the Chief" or "Thanks for the Memories."

When a Presidential election is decided by hanging chads in Florida and Al Sharpton loses weight while gaining stature in a Puerto Rican prison, we live in funny times.

Our Bill (Clinton) gave us years of unrelieved yuks. When I see him, I don't know whether to hum "Hail to the Chief" or "Thanks for the Memories."

I just happen to be one of those fortunate few who get paid to point and laugh. My life would have been a lot different if that scene in the lunchroom had ended differently. The world isn't nearly as funny when viewed through eyes swollen shut by blunt force.

But today, to quote the late Lou Gehrig, I feel like the luckiest man in the world.

And I owe it all to Bob.

'Are you anybody?':
So much for fame (Minus 14 minutes and 56 seconds)

Andy Warhol once promised that each of us would be famous for 15 minutes.

I'm returning the unused portion of my time.

Which, if you subtract how long it took me to deliver my line in "Rocky V," leaves 14 minutes and 56 seconds to divide among you.

I can't recall precisely what my line was.

Not that it wasn't memorable, but when you're caught up in the warming flush of fleeting fame, details escape you.

My line may not have been as memorable as "Frankly, Scarlett, I don't give a damn," but it was much more pivotal than "Where to, Mac?"

Besides, it was my line.

I had spent hours getting just the right intonation. I hit my mark (that's movie talk) repeatedly over the 12 hours of shooting it took to get our three-minute scene into the can (another technical term).

I was told more than once that my performance was a tour de force – the four most important seconds in the film.

I was also told to hold on to my day job.

But it wasn't the sarcastic stabs of envious friends that made me question this whole fame thing.

And it certainly wasn't the loss of privacy – which is too often a necessary trade-off for people whose lives are played out in the public arena.

page 31

What frustrated me most about my moment of fame is that no one noticed it was my moment. I had to wedge my way into the public arena.

Stargazers who lined Chestnut Street outside Sam's Place – site of the premiere – all seemed distracted when I entered. So did the crowd that was shoehorned into the post-premiere party at the Warwick.

They were looking for larger luminaries, the Stallones, the Shires. Even Burt Young would do.

I figured they hadn't braved high winds and traffic snarls just for me, but I wasn't expecting this attitude of "Yo, what's this dim light doing in our constellation of stars?"

A friend had offered to stand in the crowd and shout "Hey, ain't that Elmer Smith?" as I stepped from the limo onto the red carpet.

Not a bad idea. It just didn't seem necessary.

Turns out it wouldn't have worked anyway.

Due to the press of events, we didn't get to the premiere until after they had rolled up the red carpet.

Thursday is my wife's bowling night. Her teammates wouldn't let her bowl out.

By the time she changed from her bowling shoes into her heels, the strobe lights had cooled.

We ended up parking the Honda three blocks away and walking to the theater.

Then they let us walk right in without showing our coveted VIP passes – not because we were VIPs but because nobody seemed to notice us.

It got worse.

After the movie, we walked to the post-premiere party at Polo Bay, the disco at the Warwick.

If it hadn't been for Daily News man-about-town Stu Bykofsky, we might still be in line.

We all but sneaked into an area of the club that they had roped off for VIPs. This was a mistake.

Autograph seekers got real annoyed when they had to elbow past me to get to people like Charles Barkley, Meldrick Taylor and Big Al Meltzer.

I took a perverse pleasure in that.

"That wasn't anybody, was it?" one woman asked.

page 32

"Nah, I don't think so," her friend answered after searching my face.

Worse were the people who came right up with autograph pads poised, and asked me whether I was anybody.

Hard to know how to answer that one.

This one lady almost made the whole night worthwhile, though.

I saw her whispering to a friend before she finally approached me.

"I've been reading your column for years," she said. "I love your writing."

"Thank you so much," I said with maybe a little too much gratitude.

"Oh no. Thank you, Claude" she said triumphantly.

I guess I should have corrected her. Claude Lewis is a good 30 or 40 years older than I am.

But I didn't want to ruin her moment. Mine was already shot.

– November 20, 1990

Another Elmer passes through

Think twice before using this column as a dart board. You literally could deface a famous person.

How famous?

Would you believe famous enough to have a stone monument named for me in Wilkes-Barre?

It came up kind of suddenly two weeks ago. I was an overnight guest in the home of a young man named Jimmy Clark whom I consider kind of special.

Clark is a freshman at Wilkes College and the sports editor of the Beacon, Wilkes' college daily. I have been keeping an eye on him since he was a high school junior covering boxing matches in Atlantic City for the Ocean City Sentinel-Ledger.

He was the youngest credentialed reporter I ever met in a boxing press room. I was impressed. He had decided early that he wanted to be a sports writer and he wasn't waiting to work toward that goal.

To see someone working long and hard to get to where you are makes you realize how lucky you are to be there.

So, I gave him my phone number and told him to call on me if he ever needed me.

The call came in March. All he wanted me to do was to make the 3 1/2-hour drive from my home in New Jersey to Wilkes College by 9 on a Friday morning to deliver a 15-minute speech to a group of high school students.

Furthermore, he would prefer to have me there on Thursday night so that I could meet with a group of Beacon staffers. To keep me from getting bogged down in figuring my fee, he told there would be none. Nor could the Beacon afford to put me up in a hotel. But he was certain his parents could make room for me.

Naturally, I jumped at the opportunity.

The family prepared a place for me at his table and was waiting for me to arrive Thursday evening when Jimmy's sister, Camille, an honor student at Bishop O'Reilly High School, was stricken with severe abdominal pains.

Somewhere in Luzerne County, this writer has been commemorated in stone.

She was rushed to the hospital just before I arrived and was detained overnight. Camille and her mother, Judy, who spent the night beside her at the Geisinger Medical Center, left the house to me, Jim Clark Sr., Jimmy and the brothers, Bret and Joe.

I never got to meet Camille. But the following day, when I called back to thank the Clarks for their hospitality, I learned what a great impact my visit had had on the missing Camille.

"Sorry I didn't get to spend more time with you," Judy Clark said. "Camille is really sorry she didn't get to meet you. But the good news is she is going to be fine.

"She passed a kidney stone early this morning. And she named it Elmer in your honor."

So there. All you detractors and slow converts be advised.

Somewhere in Luzerne County, this writer has been commemorated in stone.

– April 27, 1989

Smooth, not rough:
Caleye would be appalled at today's poolrooms

I could see from the parking lot that the Cue Club in Mt. Laurel, N.J., was not very much like the poolrooms of my youth.

First off, everything going on inside was visible from 20 yards away, through big plate-glass windows. Proprietors and patrons at the places I used to play didn't encourage long-distance surveillance.

Most poolrooms were either upstairs over something, downstairs under something or through the backdoor of something.

The old Pearl Street poolroom was different. It was on the ground floor, near Haddington Recreation Center at 57th Street and Haverford Avenue, in West Philadelphia.

But you had to go through an alley to get to it. Some guys would just as soon pass up a chance to play as to venture back there.

Most poolrooms had these tiny signs generally with one word on them: POOL or BILLIARDS.

I used to go to sleep to the clicking of the balls at the Race Street poolroom. I didn't know what was making that sound until I was in junior high school.

OK, so I wasn't too swift. But I wasn't the only kid around 52d and Race Sts. who didn't know a poolroom was behind that big wooden door up those stairs.

page 36

We weren't supposed to know.

You had to be 18 to go into the poolrooms.

And even that may not have been enough time to get ready for some of what went on inside.

Pool wasn't the only game played in poolrooms.

It wasn't too surprising to run into a craps game on occasion - an occasion like, oh say, sunset.

First place I ever saw the late Sonny Liston was in a craps game on the front table at Pearl Street.

And while he might have struck terror in Floyd Patterson's heart, there were guys in Pearl Street who would try him if he grabbed the wrong pot.

Not that you had to be a tough guy to make the most out of your time in the poolrooms.

In fact, the guys who seemed to fare best were smooth rather than rough.

One of my favorites was a guy we called "Caleye," which was short for California Max.

Caleye was beyond smooth. He had the most friction-free surface I ever saw on a human.

He rarely raised his voice, and even though his clothes didn't seem especially expensive, everything seemed to fit as though it was made on him.

He wore a diamond pinky piece that would cut up under the table lights when he formed his bridge.

But it was more about flair than style. One guy, named Henry Jafar, seldom wore anything more expensive than an Army field jacket.

But Jafar wore a black patch over an empty eye socket, had a beard when only beatniks wore them, preferred Turkish cigarettes, and seldom smiled.

He was the most exotic-looking character I had seen at the time, and one of the best players in town.

I'd sit in the blue haze of cigarette smoke for hours watching guys like Caleye and Jafar make shots I didn't believe could be made.

Like most individual sports, pool is played over a much wider range of skills than people on the bottom of that range can ever believe.

For years, there were enough non-believers to make pool profitable for top players and entertaining for guys like me who learned the hard way that you watch some people and play others.

I spent hours watching George the Dragon, Rotation Slim, Chester Leroy, Machine Gun Butera, Jimmy Fusco and Harry "The Golden Greek" Petros.

These were real people - some at least as good as TV pool idols like Steve Mizerak.

But their skills were on display only behind closed doors, upstairs or downstairs or in backrooms where people paid to see how good they were.

Last Saturday, I played eight ball and straight pool with my daughter, while my granddaughter ran between the Cue Club's 22 brass-accented tables.

I couldn't have done that 25 years ago.

"Housewives bring babies in strollers," said co-owner George Markovich. "Whole families come in."

In Manhattan, yuppie businessmen in $1,000 suits play in luxurious pool parlors.

I guess it's a long overdue change.

But I can't help wondering what a guy like Caleye could do in a place like that.

– November 6, 1990

'Gimme a hightop fade': Tonsorial tradition just ain't what it used to be

I'm in the barbershop waiting for my monthly haircut when it occurs to me that they've been treating me like a stepchild long enough.

No, I mean it this time. I'm not taking it any more!

I'm not getting stuck in another tonsorial traffic tie-up behind a long line of young brothers with double-figure hat sizes, not without standing up for my rights and the rights of my kind!

My kind is the growing legion of balding brothers who silently suffer second-class treatment.

I'm talking about guys who were regular patrons when electric clippers were a new-fangled novelty.

The new elite in today's barbershops are young guys whose custom cuts require as much care as a Palm Beach lawn.

It's bad enough that they've changed the whole mood of the barber shop.

It used to be a place where guys got together to talk about sports or to lie about the women they imagined having.

Some of the most outrageous yarns ever spun from the mouths of men started from thin threads of truth that grew to mythic proportions before my very ears.

Back then, we young guys took a number, sat down and shut up.

The little baldie haircut our mothers made us get took about five quick clipper swipes.

page 39

The barber handled your head as though your body weren't attached to it. Hair fell in clumps onto your bib.

And you were done – quicker than Mothers Oats.

The barber threw up a cloud of Jeris Talc, and passed a mirror in front of your face so fast you couldn't have seen yourself if the cloud had cleared.

But even with that bum's rush, I could still spend half a day listening to lies because there were always some adults who absolutely had to get into the chair before me – even though I had the lower number.

Sometimes they got out of the chair and stood around talking for the next half hour.

But I was taught not to notice.

We had respect for our elders back then.

So what did it get us? OK, so we did get to ogle the JET magazine centerfold a little longer.

But now that it's our turn to tell the lies and bully the young guys, they won't stand for it.

Whatever happened to tradition, respect for elders, my turn in the seat of power?

I was taught not to notice the guys who were playing numbers, buying illegal Irish Sweepstakes tickets or engaging in that occasional transaction in "hot" (sometimes piping hot) merchandise.

We had respect for our elders back then.

So what did it get us?

OK, so we did get to ogle the Jet Magazine centerfold a little longer.

But now that it's our turn to tell the lies and bully the young guys, they won't stand for it.

Whatever happened to tradition, respect for elders, my turn in the seat of power?

Instead, all I get is tired.

I'm tired of watching young guys come in and spend as much time just explaining what they want done as it takes to cut what's left of my hair.

"Ahh, give me a hightop fade with three parts on the left, two parts on the right," I hear them say.

I see guys ask to have their girlfriend's initials cut into the back of heads large enough to accommodate her full name and phone number.

I heard a guy ask for a "Gumby." And the barber not only knew what it was but clipped his hair into a perfect high-on-one-side low-on-the other asymetrical style.

At least the guy behind him at the movies that night could get an obstructed view of the screen. A lot of us don't get to see anything but some bozo's girlfriend's initials.

I'm tired of waiting while two or three barbers confer over one head as if some delicate surgical procedure was about to take place.

I'm tired of having to wait while Junior rises to his full height to lean over in the mirror and carefully inspect every inch of acreage as if his head was a relief map of some important military objective.

I'm tired enough to do something about it - and I would, too, except that some of these youngsters are so large the barber never has to jack the chair up.

Just once, I'd like to see somebody jack one of them up.

It won't be me, though. I'm afraid I'd end up being the jackee.

In fact, I wouldn't even be writing this if I thought some of these fine young men would read the editorial section.

They don't, do they?

– *March 6, 1990*

Wildwood casino: Snake eyes for tribe

We've got a team of genealogists sifting through a Hefty bag full of birth records and Smith family artifacts in search of our Native American roots.

So far, all they've turned up is a distant cousin with high cheekbones who is believed to have worn moccasins to a family gathering. But the search continues. The stakes are too high for my people to leave this stone unturned.

Because, unless the feds kick in that 40 acres and a mule we were promised (with interest), my best shot to reap a bonanza from an ancestry of oppression is to get in on this Indian casino thing.

If the mayor of Wildwood can suddenly discover 1,200 acres of Indian ancestral lands in the middle of town, I should be able to find a couple of drops of Indian blood coursing through my veins.

Mayor Fred Wager (five'll get you 10 that's not his real name) is proposing to turn over this plot of prime real estate to members of the Delaware Nation. To hear him tell it, 1,200 displaced Delawares, now living in Anadarko, Okla., have longed to return to their ancestral lands by the sea.

For generations, hizzoner would have us believe, Delaware elders have regaled their young with tales of ancestral exploits along the South Jersey shoreline – the wind, the waves, the saltwater taffy. And now, the Delawares' dream of a return to Cape May County may soon be realized.

page 42

Or maybe not. Not if Donald Trump, Merv Griffin and Steve Wynn have any say. And with Gov. Christie Todd Whitman hauling water for them in Trenton – they will have their say.

And for once, I find myself firmly in their camp. But it's not because I support Atlantic City's God-given right to be the only Jersey shore community licensed to fleece suckers by the busload.

I'm running with the big dogs on this one because Fred Wager's gambling gambit is the slimiest pile of refuse to wash up on the Jersey shore since those syringes beached themselves near Asbury Park a couple of years back.

It marks a near-perfect union of governmental hypocrisy and cynicism. It's another brick in that firm foundation of lies and half-truths America's gaming industry has built its house on. Everything about it rings as hollow as a slug in a slot machine.

Whether it's the creative accounting that allows casinos to rake in billions and pay taxes on millions or just the basic myth that you can deal with the devil without risking your soul, it's all shrouded in a thin tissue of lies.

On the Mississippi they call it riverboat gambling to evoke the imagery of a bucolic past. In reality, the truly rich investors can just spit on the ground, call it a river, and build a boat.

They live with whatever regulations the locals impose until they can get a better deal. When the state of Mississippi offered easier regulations three years ago, the four boats along Iowa's Mississippi shores headed south so fast you could water-ski behind them.

But the hypocrisy of garden-variety gaming multiplies exponentially when it's cleverly coupled with America's long history of Indian exploitation. That's what makes this Wildwood thing so special.

In a lame attempt to keep pace with the seaside shlock next door, Wildwood would cash in on the Indian Gaming Regulatory Act of 1988 – a law which has done little to improve the lot of most tribes.

page 43

Because of the media's persistent focus on a few well-heeled tribes whose riches rise from an anomaly in the law, the truth about the relatively meager revenues that Native Americans have reaped from this "bonanza" and the stringent regulations they operate under are little known.

Reports like CBS' "60 Minutes" recent "Wampum Wonderland" segment focus on one or two tribes such as the Meshantucket Pequots in Connecticut.

Because their tribe is so small and its population center is so large, they have managed to take in enough money so that, even after money is allotted to the educational and social services uses mandated under the law, they still had enough left to split amongst tribal members.

They also donated $100 million to the state, which has no taxing authority over them.

You can bet dollars to donuts you won't see Merv and the Don doing that.

What's more common is barely-solvent bingo halls along desolate stretches of Indian-land in one of the plains states.

"This focus on a few rich tribes hurts the majority of Indians," said Thomas Sweeney, a spokesman for the U.S. Bureau of Indian Affairs.

That false perception has becomes the reality used to justify heavy-handed cuts in the Indian Affairs appropriation in the current Senate budget bill.

"The Senate bill would cut $434 million from the ($1.9 billion) Clinton appropriation for Indian affairs," Sweeney said. "They cut $30 million from education funding alone.

"That would devastate the tribes. Ada Deer (head of the Indian affairs bureau and assistant secretary of Indian Affairs) calls it termination by appropriation."

I think I'm going to call off the roots search.

And if the Delawares are as smart as I hope they are, they'll turn their backs to this wind from the East and be glad they got out when they did.

– August 16, 1995

page 44

Can't count on shipyard to be around in long run

We called it "the Yard" - this place where my dad spent every working day for 40-some years.

I wasn't sure what he did at "the Yard," but every once in a while he'd complain about the ladders he had to climb. I was 10 or 12 when I realized his job classification was boilermaker and climbing ladders between decks and in the massive boilers that powered the huge warships they built at the yard was just an occupational hazard.

So was the asbestos that killed hundreds of shipyard workers, especially boilermakers. They'd contract something called asbestosis, which progressed into lung cancer and death. For years, even after that threat and other occupational hazards were well-documented, hundreds of men like my father ignored the risks and went to the shipyards every day.

Because it was a good job. Men like my father who did not have much education or many marketable skills could buy houses, raise families and claim their small piece of the American dream because they worked at the yard.

I think about it a lot lately, with all the talk of reopening the old Philadelphia Naval Shipyard at the foot of Broad Street. I think about going to ballgames at Connie Mack Stadium with my dad and how we would invariably run into other shipyard workers with their sons. They called him Smitty, and they were Jonesey or Browney – everybody at the yard seemed to have a name that ended with a "y" sound.

I remember the first time I saw the yard. It was 1959, I had won a Union League boys citizenship award, and one of the day's activities was a trip to the Navy Yard. We boarded a submarine and had lunch aboard the USS Kitty Hawk, the largest Navy aircraft carrier at the time.

"My father works here," I must have said to every boy on our bus at some point. I wanted them to know that I had a father and he had a good job.

At the yard.

He had been retired for 20 years when he died 12 years ago. I didn't think about the yard or what it meant to me anymore until the city and state started dangling hundreds of millions of dollars to lure a foreign firm in to reopen the yard.

And in the throes of the nostalgia that the negotiations evoked, I forgot about why the Navy Yard and the New York shipbuilding works across the river in Camden and a dozen other public and private shipyards had closed.

I forgot that in the new global economy the "good living" my father and men like him made in the shipyards isn't always viewed as a good thing.

In shipyards in Korea, where people earn less money for the same work, and where the government will subsidize steel production to lure business, costs have been cut to where it's hard for us to compete.

I forgot that America is in the business of business and American business magnates can make as many billions investing in shipyards and steel mills overseas as they can building their own.

Maybe a lot of us whose futures were built on the strong backs of men and women in mills and yards forgot that and invested a little too much hope in the $430 million deal, which is still expected to bring Kvaerner ASA to the foot of Broad Street. Some of us got a rude awakening from our nostalgia this week when Kvaerner succumbed to the trend that closed our yards and mills years ago.

It's going to be OK, our leaders tell us. The deal was structured with the big picture in mind. Someone will step in and reopen our yard if Kvaerner backs out.

page 46

And that may be. But other voices, ominous voices, tell us that the network of suppliers and subcontractors needed to support this enterprise are not in place and may never be.

They say that the U.S. government has yet to demonstrate the determination to give American industrialists the tools they need to meet the aggressive competition with subsidized industries in such places as Korea. And they say the trend that has driven Americans and Europeans out of business is irreversible, even if the U.S. government issues strong trade sanctions.

I don't know who to believe. But I think it's time we looked at redirecting the $350 million in public money that remains and consider using it to draw in some of the high-tech, information-age industries that American workers and businessmen can expect to control well into the future.

Folks like me will always remember fondly an era of America's supremacy in shipbuilding and steel-making and other industries where men and women with little education and few marketable skills could find a "good job."

But you can't base public policy on nostalgia.

– *April 16, 1999*

Laughing at black humor: Television's "In Living Color" marks a coming of age

A few of my heavier colleagues and I were charting the evolution of black society in America when I stumbled upon the single most important index of black progress.

One guy said we made our most significant step as a people when we went from being property to owning property.

No. That's not it, somebody else said. It was when we moved from enforced illiteracy to a point where many of us have become noted scholars.

Another great thinker pointed out that our evolution as citizens wasn't complete until we fought for and won the right to vote and went on to win high elective offices.

The correct answer, I informed my colleagues, is "(D.) None of the above."

Owning property is certainly significant, I agreed. There's nothing like having your own slice of the American pie to certify your citizenship claim.

And it was surely a long hard road that took us from our ABC's to our Ph.D's.

But that, I counseled my colleagues, ain't it either.

History will show that our coming of age as a people in America can be marked on a scale that runs from "Amos 'n' Andy" to "In Living Color."

Or, more precisely, from the absence of "Amos 'n' Andy" to "In Living Color."

Because in the 30 years or so since the NAACP ran Andy and the Kingfish out of town on a rail, we have learned to laugh at ourselves – in public.

page 48

True progress for black folks is reflected in the fact that we are now confident enough in who we are to let the world in on our inside jokes.

Black folks have always laughed about things they would not find funny in mixed company.

Back when he was still funny, Dick Gregory used to talk about it in his nightclub act.

"If I said the things about black people that you say, you'd be hurt," a white man told him once.

"Not so," Gregory told him. "If you said those things, you'd get hurt."

I learned it by "playing the dozens," which means telling insulting jokes about each other's mothers.

I played the dozens so well I could talk about the mothers of the baddest dudes in schools.

But I had to be good enough to make them laugh before they made me cry.

Today, after years of gaudy accomplishments have proved we are not all shiftless (whatever that is) and lazy, it's okay to point out that some of us are.

And, yes, some of the black folks in jail are where they ought to be.

It does not diminish us as a people to take a humorous look at some of these things.

It certainly has not diminished Keenan Ivory Wayans, who will reap millions as the creator, producer and chief writer of "In Living Color."

If black Americans were offended by George "Kingfish" Stevens' weekly swindles of the slow-talking, slow-witted Andrew H. Brown, there's no telling what would have happened if "In Living Color" had hit the airwaves 30 years ago.

We would have worn out a pair of shoes each marching on whatever we had to march on.

What has caused this change? Well, Wayans may have touched on the key point in an interview on "20/20" last week.

It's OK for him to spoof black crime the way his "homeboy shopping network" segments do or to ridicule black homosexuals the way his "men on art" skits do because it is a show by blacks about blacks.

Maybe. But it takes a little getting used to for guys like me who came up when that kind of humor was kept behind tightly closed doors.

I went to see Wayans' "I'm Gonna Get You, Sucka" in a suburban mall outside South Bend, Indiana.

I laughed in the dark at scenes which showed a ghetto olympics with events like an auto-stripping contest and the hundred-yard stolen appliance dash.

But I was sensitive to every comment I overheard as I walked out in an otherwise all-white crowd.

In the final analysis, what makes it work is something I learned back at Shoemaker Junior High.

I learned it by "playing the dozens," which means telling insulting jokes about each other's mothers.

I played the dozens so well I could talk about the mothers of the baddest dudes in schools.

But I had to be good enough to make them laugh before they made me cry.

Therein lies the real secret of "In Living Color."

You can get away with saying almost anything about almost anybody – as long as it's funny enough.

– September 13, 1990

Chapter 3

Food fights

Vegetarians are killers, too

In my family, we gather the children for the ritual slaying of the Thanksgiving turkey.

And not just any anonymous turkey. It has to be a gobbler that the little ones have raised themselves, usually a pet that has eaten out of their hands or waddled to the edge of the pen to greet them when they came home from school. There are no strangers at our table on Thanksgiving.

Nothing whets the appetite like running down the little critter or watching feathers fly as we take turns plucking our catch. Sure, it can be a little traumatic for the youngest members of the family.

But it could be worse. They could be on the other end of the food chain.

That's the way we do it in our family. But it's OK with us if your family does it another way.

We just don't want to hear about it.

We don't want to know that you don't touch anything other than organically grown vegetables or that your salads are made with uncultivated field greens. We do know that a turkey is one of God's creatures. But God's creatures have been feeding on each other since creation. It's in his plan.

If you choose to follow another plan, that's OK, too. But spare us the sanctimony and the scare tactics. I'm never going to start a guilt trip on an empty stomach.

Some of us happen to feel that vegetarianism is barbaric. I'm not trying to hear an ethics lesson from someone who would cut the eyes out of a potato and then mash it to a pulp.

What could be sadder than the sight of a beautiful floret of broccoli buried under a scalding stream of molten cheddar? Where's all that varmint-loving compassion when they're skinning a carrot or dunking a basket of sliced potatoes in boiling oil?

You can't drive more than a few miles without passing a sign from People for the Ethical Treatment of Animals reminding us that Thanksgiving is tough on Turkeys. Well, it's also rough on rutabagas.

Vegetables are living things, too. I hope the People for the Ethical Treatment of Animals will consider that before they boil a head of cabbage or an ear of corn or jab an elbow of macaroni with a fork.

You can't drive more than a few miles without passing a sign from People for the Ethical Treatment of Animals reminding us that Thanksgiving is tough on Turkeys. Well, it's also rough on rutabagas.

I just wish the doomsayers at the Centers for Disease Control, the American Council on Science and Health and all the other hermetically sealed environs where people in starched lab coats are paid to furrow their brows and issue warnings to the rest of us would take the day off.

I'm not sure when this Thanksgiving tradition got started, but it seems like everybody who has ever peered at a petri dish through a microscope has chosen this season to issue their ominous tidings.

It's the annual microbe alert, a time when the scientists serve up heaping portions of paranoia for our own good.

It's bad enough that the Journal of the American Medical Association is prohibited by law from publishing an edition that doesn't contain at least one study revealing that something we eat, wear or breathe on a regular basis is lethal to laboratory rats. Billions of dollars in research grants are spent finding new ways to kill rats.

page 54

My wife has a theory about these things. She says it's like one of the basic laws of physics: anything you start to enjoy will set off an equal and opposite reaction in a lab or within some group of tree-huggers or other lovers of non-human living things.

Sex is out. It was always discouraged. But when they told us it would make us blind, we covered one eye and risked the other. Now, it can kill you.

You can't eat, wear or sleep with anything that has ever lived. So what's left?

Well for us, there is the annual turkey slaughter for which we are most thankful. We are committed carnivores in our family.

But for all you tree-hugging, cloth-coat-wearing vegetarians out there – we'll lift a drumstick for you if you'll hoist a bean sprout for us.

– November 25, 1998

Where do soul-food lovers end up? Hog heaven

One of the oddest things about the holidays is the way families gather to eat traditional ethnic foods that some of them wouldn't even throw at each other the rest of the year.

Risking heartburn with loved ones is a cherished tradition in most cultures, one which has resisted the homogenizing process of Americanization.

Some of the stuff is not all that bad for you. Italians get together on Christmas Eve for seven kinds of fish. Except for the heightened risk of mercury poisoning and an occasional seafood OD, it's a fairly healthy tradition.

But then they follow it with enough canolis and chianti to negate the value of the fish.

A Hanukkah favorite are latkes, which is a kind of starchy potato pancake cooked in heavy oil and covered with a glob of sour cream. And for any celebrant who hasn't had his fill of cooking lubricants after a few of these depth charges, there's always sufganiyot, which is a deep-fried donut.

And for a heartstopper any time of year, it's hard to beat schmaltz, which is chicken fat that has been rendered so it can be poured over other foods. (And then there is gribenes, the cracklins from the schmaltz.)

Slavic families gather on Christmas Eve for pierogi dripping in butter. Later, they sit and listen to each others' arteries close.

This is the kind of ethnic fare that keeps cardiologists in BMWs.

page 56

But there is no holiday tradition that clogs as many arteries as Southern cooking. Southern cooks employ lard and bacon grease in more ways than cooks from other regions can imagine.

Who else could have come up with the idea of dipping a perfectly good steak in batter, deep-frying it into submission and calling it chicken fried steak?

But if plain ol' Southern cooking is dangerous, soul food, its swaggering offshoot, is positively death-defying. Theoretically, it's possible to cook soul food without pork. I've seen it done. My mother-in-law seasons her collard greens with smoked turkey wings. Except for the obvious absence of floating hog meat, you can hardly tell the difference.

Not all departures from traditional form work that well, however. Usually you sacrifice flavor when you depork your recipes.

Our own cafeteria here in the Great White Tower of Truth prepares blackeyed peas without ham hocks, for instance. If you smash them with your fork, they make a great paste for hanging Christmas cards.

But they do not make great soul food.

What makes great soul food is cholesterol. Cholesterol is not sold separately like batteries. If it were, it would carry the following warning label: Eat at your own risk, cholesterol kills.

But cholesterol doesn't come in a box. For us soul-food devotees, cholesterol comes packed in pigs.

A little bit of the culinary history of my people is necessary here. As you may know, our Southern ancestors learned by necessity to do more with pig parts than George Washington Carver did with peanuts.

They didn't serve pork butter and jelly sandwiches. But they did rival Carver for inventiveness in the use of a food product.

There are, for instance, a dozen ways to serve pigs' feet that qualify as soul food. And there are at least as many ways to cook pig tails, pig snouts, pig ears, hogs' heads and hog maws (for those unfamiliar with pork, hog maws are not the opposite of hog paws).

page 57

Soul food gives us a number of ways to prepare pork parts that were once thought to be inedible, including hog guts or chitlins (a/k/a ``chitterlings'') and a low-on-the-hog delicacy called mountain oysters, which are neither seafood nor mountain fare.

I'd really rather not say what they are. But I can tell you that once they're removed, the average pig loses his will to live.

As incredible as this now seems, mountain oysters, hog brains and chitlins used to be routinely thrown out by people who didn't even realize they were food.

"Hog brains and eggs are the caviar of soul food," my friend Bob Williams told me once. Chitlin lovers would argue that point, although most modern, urban blacks have somehow lost their taste for hog intestines. Go figure.

The standard way to cook chitlins is to turn them inside out, rip off the fat that grows inside and clean them with a wire brush. Then you simmer them for hours along with some cut-up maws.

There are variations. Eddie Campbell, a trustee at my church, told me about a little-known favorite, French-fried chitlins. Sounds like a clash of cultures. But I understand it's delicious.

Before you turn up your nose, remember some of you wolf down bags of pork rinds, which are deep-fried hog hides. It's a favorite of our president, Bill Clinton, who is known to favor foods that kill.

All of this comes up, of course, because we are well into the holiday season when many of us will be sharing steaming servings of fatal food with loved ones.

My family and, no doubt, the Clintons will spend New Year's eating collard greens and hoppin' John, which is black-eyed peas over rice. In the Southern tradition, hoppin' John is eaten for good luck and greens for money.

They bring more gas than good luck. But traditions don't die easy.

So eat up. And as they say down home, bon appetit, y'all.

– December 18, 1996

page 58

Chicken on the range
Nothing to fear but government's health bulletins

I think it was right after the "Rocky the Range Chicken" controversy that I finally gave myself permission to ignore the government's regular health scare bulletins.

I had always wondered whether the government could ever save enough lives to make up for the people they have scared to death.

Who'll ever forget the panic we were thrown into when some diligent inspector found traces of cyanide in a couple of Chilean grapes?

Entire nations teetered on the brink of economic ruin as we held up flotillas of South American cargo ships on the high seas. Imagine the tax dollars it took to finance a crew large enough to inspect individual grapes!

The all-clear was finally sounded after government experts ascertained that the human stomach can't hold enough cyanide-laced grapes to risk a person's life.

Then there was the time some keen-eyed citizen reported seeing a critter that fit the description of a Mediterranean fruit fly cross the Mexican border into California. The U.S. Department of Agriculture responded by unleashing a blizzard of insecticides on the orchards of Southern California.

On the positive side, the "med fly" hasn't been seen since. But you'd probably be safer eating cyanide-laced Chilean grapes than the fruit that lived through that spray storm of "safe" insecticides.

page 59

There was at least the distant risk that our lives – or the quality of our lives – were at risk in those cases. But I couldn't see any justification for the heavy-handed government regulation that almost cost Rocky the Range Chicken his identity.

This started two months ago when the U.S. Department of Agriculture prohibited a California chicken rancher from using the term "range chickens" to describe his poultry.

Bart Ehman, the poultry producer who came up with the name, said he uses it in advertising because his chickens are allowed to roam the range freely in a "stress-free" environment.

A spokesman for Agriculture's food safety inspection service explained to the Wall Street Journal that the government decided to prohibit the ad campaign because "We don't have a working definition for 'range' . . . What is a range in the regulatory sense?"

They lifted the "Rocky statute" several weeks later after a compliance investigation verified that Ehman's chickens do have access to a range. He is still prohibited from claiming his chickens live in a "stress-free environment".

But the whole controversy was so ridiculous that it freed me from a lot of the stress I used to feel at the sound of this phrase: "the U.S. Department of Agriculture today said . . .'."

No longer will my peace of mind be threatened by reports of laboratory rats dying, their little bellies bloated by massive quantities of some substance that probably wouldn't have killed them if they hadn't been forced to eat so much of it.

Take Red Dye No 3. The Food and Drug Administration banned the substance used to color maraschino cherries, after 15 of the 70 male rats that were fed large doses of it developed tumors.

FDA admits that the amount of coloring used in the test would be the equivalent of a human eating 724,700 cans of fruit cocktail with colored cherries every year for life.

But they are required, Health and Human Services Secretary Louis Sullivan explained, to act against even the most remote risk of cancer.

Then there is the continuing controversy about the effects of cholesterol on the heart and the effects of certain foods on cholesterol – none of which will have any effect on me.

page 60

Thanks to the Rocky the Range Chicken controversy, I never joined my health-conscious colleagues who risked oat-bran overdoses in what turns out to be a futile effort to cut cholesterol levels.

After several "scientific" studies which purported to show that oat bran could unclog your arteries, the New England Journal of Medicine published a work by researchers from the Harvard Medical School.

Their study showed that the oat bran eaters from earlier studies had benefited from eating fewer fatty foods – not more fiber.

Don't get me wrong, though. I wouldn't urge you to woof down Chilean grapes with maraschino chasers, but until they come up with the definitive study, I'll remember Rocky the Range Chicken and take my health bulletins with a grain of salt.

– *April 17, 1990*

Stop the
(cell) madness

Let me say here that I oppose dragging inconsiderate cell-phone users to their death over razor-sharp spikes.

At least I do this week.

But I've got about one more time to be startled from my reverie in a darkened theater or one more time to overhear the semi-private blatherings of some wireless nitwit before I join the secret society for the ritual slaying of the self-indulgent.

Please don't ask for their e-mail address.

They are, after all, a secret society.

At least they are this week.

But the cell-phone backlash is building to a fever pitch in this country, and even peace-loving, law-abiding live-and-let-live types like us are starting to ponder the possibility of sacrificing one or two of these cell simpletons on TV.

At least it would give them something to say in their next wireless transmission. So far, all we overhear in these stage-whispered conversations sounds about like this:

"So, I'm like. . .and she's like. . .

"So, I go. . .and then he goes. . ."

After about five minutes of this banal banter, I'm like, "Hey, bozo, ring this."

You'll be pleased to know (or maybe not) that I stifled that very reaction two weeks ago. I was in a movie theater watching Kevin Spacey throw his dinner across the dining room when some VIP two rows in front of me received an incoming call.

page 62

I'm expecting Dr. What's-His-Name to rush out, black bag in hand, to attend a patient on the brink of death. No such luck.

Instead, I hear a whispering voice describing the movie scene for the person on the other end of the line. In the old days, I could have summoned an usher. But there are no ushers in these multiplex theaters, just victims in darkened boxes.

A few seconds later, it stopped. I didn't know whether someone strangled the person in the dark. And I didn't care.

That's what it's coming to. I don't care what happens to them anymore.

For instance, I can't see banning the use of cell phones while driving. It doesn't seem any worse than watching women apply makeup between lights or guys steer with one hand and watch the road with one eye while leaning over to look for something in the glove box.

But when the subject came up in an editorial board meeting, I just sat there with a little grin. I don't like this about myself. But it's where I am today.

I should have seen this coming. Eight years ago, my wife and I were on vacation in Vancouver, British Columbia. Every restaurant had a notice on the menu saying cell phones were prohibited.

"Why?" I asked the waiter.

He just shrugged.

But then I noticed what I'd soon see back home. Looked like the whole town was unwired. In the hotel lobby, on the streets, at every bus stop, people were talking into cell phones instead of to each other.

This was back in the flip-phone era. That's when relatively few people had them. They used to make a show of flipping them out in an arrogant gesture that seemed to say: "I've got one, and you don't."

Those were the good old days before they spread like a rampant virus in a kind of electronic cell division. Now, everyone has at least one, sometimes in Crayola colors.

They're making them smaller and smaller. You see them on people's belt loops. Some are so small it looks like people are talking into their hands.

But they are no less annoying as multi-colored miniatures than they were when they were larger and grayer. It's still none of my business what you are cooking for dinner tonight – and I'd just as soon not hear it on the subway ride home.

It won't be long before some seemingly sane commuter or theater patron will finally be pushed over the edge. It will probably happen in New York, where people barely tolerate each other anyway.

It was in New York that Laurence Fishburne had to interrupt a Shakespearean soliloquy and, in the voice of Othello, demand that some bozo hang up a cell phone.

It will be in New York that some Son of Sam goes berserk on a bus and perforates a guy who is found still clutching his tiny, purple phone, his fingers straining to dial the last digit in 911.

But nobody wants to see this wanton waste of human life.

At least, not this week.

– April 12, 2000

Cloning poses threat to male delivery

This couldn't wait for Father's Day. Those of us of the male persuasion could be obsolete by then.

Our link in the biological chain is quickly being replaced by test tubes and tissue scrapings. Only God knows what other technologies hasten our obsolescence.

They're cloning critters from body parts. Dolly the embraceable ewe was born of a union of cells matcd in a petri dish in Scotland. Researchers can't say whether the earth moved for either cell. But I can tell you, it wasn't as good for me as it was for them.

Not that anyone asked. In fact, the male point of view was less important to the development of this new technology than the horse was to the invention of the automobile. The horse was at least a reference point.

But the fact that they rate engines in terms of horsepower is an acknowledgment that the male of the species should not expect from the crew in the lab coats.

Now comes this thing out of Hawaii – the, ahh, birthplace of Fibro, a male mouse billed as the first live mammal cloned from adult cells that do not originate in the reproductive system. Big deal.

page 65

Forgive me if I don't hail this particular scientific advance. I have only this to say to Fibro: You're a traitor to your gender and yo mama is a petri dish.

But Ryuzo Yanagimachi and Teruhiko Wakayama, the two University of Hawaii researchers who came up with this breakthrough between surfing runs, are being lauded not as Fibro's creators, but as the inventors of something called the "Honolulu technique."

They shared this with the world in an e-mail interview, fostering still another non-contact sport.

The Honolulu technique differs from the method used by scientists in Scotland to produce Dolly in that the mouse embryos were created by clipping skin from the tail of a male mouse that was later transplanted into surrogate mother mice. Out of 274 tries, only three transferred embryos were carried to full term.

Forgive me if I don't hail this particular scientific advance. I have only this to say to Fibro: You're a traitor to your gender and yo mama is a petri dish.

Fibro was the only one who lived beyond infancy. The other mouse tail babies were all boys with black eyes like Fibro and reddish-brown fur like the mouse whose tail they were clipped from. You won't even need a tail clipping from the fathers of future fibros. All our body parts are being phased out.

A Japanese agricultural research institute claims it has cloned a calf from the ear of an adult steer. They didn't even bother to say whether it was a male calf or whether its parenting part was male.

Because the male of the species is becoming irrelevant. We're hearing more and more from women who want babies without the bother of mating with men. In the old technology, 274 tries was considered a good thing. Now, they're all trying to get down to none.

So, I'm not looking forward to the new millennium with joyful anticipation. This may be the last millennium in which the male has an essential role in the procreation of the species. The new millennium may usher in an era where the black widow spider is seen as a role model.

Not that women are safe from this technological onslaught. Their franchise also is threatened. "Our results demonstrate that cloning using adult somatic cells is not restricted to female or reproductive cells," the researchers said.

So, there it is. A few years from now there will be no fathers or, for that matter, mothers. I don't know about you, I'm not looking forward to a time when my descendants will be rushing out at the last minute to buy cards for Tube Day or Dish Day.

– June 2, 1999

Those nightmares could be real killers

The frog mucus story broke right in the nick of time. We were still reeling from the latest dispatch out of the office of depressing data: dreams may be bad for the heart.

In their continuing efforts to determine why so many Americans wake up dead, it seems scientists have isolated dreams as a possible cause of heart attacks and strokes.

Dr. Virend K. Somers of the University of Iowa shared this depressing data bit with us in an article published in the New England Journal of Medicine, which is second only to the Journal of the American Medical Association for the reporting of frightening factoids.

Dr. Somers and an enterprising team of researchers studied the heart rates of eight healthy volunteers who agreed to fall asleep under carefully controlled laboratory conditions.

They awoke to find that their lives had been threatened by the very same nervous reactions that kept their prehistoric ancestors from becoming after-dinner treats for the huge lizard-like creatures that roamed the earth a couple million years ago.

During dream sleep, they were able to show, the sympathetic nervous system is working overtime to release the stress hormones that widen the airways and clot the blood. In the process, the heart rate and pulse can double.

"When you think the body should be fast asleep," Dr. Somers reportedly said, "everything is pounding away. The sympathetic nervous system is in overdrive."

page 68

Which may explain why so many people have heart attacks and strokes just as they are getting out of bed. Researchers learned long ago that a surprisingly high number of heart attacks and strokes occur in and around bedrooms.

And they have long suspected there was more romance than reality in those stories of people who die in bed while in blissful embrace.

Dr. Somers was quick to point out that not all dreams are fatal. Many of us will continue to dream and live to tell about it, he says.

As comforting as that was to hear it didn't do a whole lot to lighten my mood.

Then I ran across the frog mucus story. It renewed my faith in the ways science and nature work hand in hand for a better world.

We have Dr. Katharine Milton, an anthropologist from the University of California at Berkley to thank for this one.

Dr. Milton, at great personal peril, smuggled the secretions back into the United States six years ago after witnessing an amazing demonstration of their healing powers in Brazil.

She had gone to Brazil to study how primitive people indigenous to remote areas of South America use their forest habitats to find food and medicine.

She couldn't help noticing the fresh burn scars that adorned the bodies of many of the Mayoruna Indians she saw returning from hunting excursions. So she asked.

They ran into the forest and "came back with . . . the most beautiful frog I'd ever seen in my life," she recalled.

To her amazement, the men poked the frog with a stick until it began to secrete a glossy substance on its skin. The hunters mixed the mucus with saliva to make a thick paste.

Then they burned themselves with a hot twig, scratched off the burned skin, and rubbed the paste into the raw wound.

"Within 5 to 10 minutes they were in dire straits," she said.

"The men vomited, their eyes and lips puffed up and they lay prostrate for about a day."

When they woke up, she said, they reported that they were able to hunt all day without rest and with little food or water.

page 69

And they said their arrows never missed.

She wasn't really sure how helpful this could be in, say, the San Francisco Bay area. But she could see right away that it merited further study.

So she kept the guys busy for the next week or so poking frogs with sticks until they had gathered enough mucus for scientists back home to study.

That was five years ago. Scientists in white lab coats have been mixing mucus in test tubes ever since.

But the intensive research finally seems to be paying off.

Scientists at the National Institutes of Health in Bethesda, Md., this week reported that they have discovered a peptide called adenoregulin in the frog secretion.

And, according to Thomas Spande, an NIH organic chemist, the presence of this peptide means the mucus may have some application in drugs to treat depression and strokes.

The data is still under study and scientists caution that it's too early to show a clear link between frog mucus and medicine.

Even after that hurdle is crossed, they're still going to have to fool around a little with the dosage and application.

Any fool can burn himself with a twig and pick the scab off. But just how much paste do you rub into the raw wound?

What's really important here is the way that these developments prove once again that there is an order in the universe.

One minute you hear your dreams can give you a stroke. The next minute you learn that frog mucus may prevent strokes.

A coincidence? I don't think so.

Anyway, I'm going to sleep like a baby tonight.

– February 5, 1993

For a new dinosaur: Jurassic parking

A comparison chart in the New York Times showed the Unimog between a conventional SUV and a Tyrannosaurus Rex.

The T-Rex and the SUV got a slight edge in fuel efficiency.

But in all of the other features that rich consumers care about, Unimog seemed far superior.

If you haven't picked up your brochure yet, Unimog is the new bloated road hog by Freightliner, a division of Daimler Benz Chrysler that is soon to be test marketed in the United States. Where else would you test-market a six-ton, 17-foot-long, 9-foot-tall luxury truck that sells for $84,000 stripped?

Where else could you find a minimum of 10,000 people who could afford to pull up to the pumps with an empty 52-gallon tank and say fill 'er up? Apparently they need to sell 10,000 of these fuel-swilling, pug-ugly monster trucks to break even next year.

No problem. As Daimler Chrysler knows all too well, it's virtually impossible to price yourself out of the U.S. market these days. In fact, prohibitive price tags are a selling point in America.

Unimog is essentially an old German military truck that can be converted into a luxury SUV for the Sunday driver who likes to roam the countryside chewing terrain like a T-Rex. As luxury toys go, this one's going to be hard to beat.

page 71

Comes with amber running lights and a chrome-plated vertical exhaust pipe that spews billowing black exhaust fumes just like the 50-foot, 18-wheel Freightliners that box us in on major highways. And there's an optional chain-activated air horn to really scare the heck out of fellow motorists.

It's got a windshield the size of a store-front window so the driver can see the little compacts scurrying around him and, most important, so they can see him.

Because, what is the point of conspicuous consumption if it is not, well, conspicuous?

I remember rushing outside the Riviera Hotel in Las Vegas with Mike Tyson one night to see his latest toy. It was a Lamborghini truck. He said he had two of them.

It's got a windshield the size of a store-front window so the driver can see the little compacts scurrying around him and, most important, so they can see him.

Because, what is the point of conspicuous consumption if it is not, well, conspicuous?

It cost more than $100,000 and looked like a warthog squatting next to the curb to do its business. I was told it would do 100 mph in desert sand, which made it all the rage for the pampered sons of sheikhs.

And I thought: It really is better to be rich.

I've been thinking that a lot lately as I read about the toys and games being sold to those consumers who want and can afford to buy the biggest, best and first.

Robin Leach didn't prepare us for this. There's stuff for sale you and I don't even know about until we read about some guy who has one. How many of us knew you could get a night in the Lincoln bed for a six-figure contribution to Bill and Hillary Clinton?

page 72

And who knew that a combination of connections and contributions could buy you a seat at the controls of a nuclear submarine on a training mission?

Last summer, someone speculated that, for a few million or so, you could reserve a place on the first passenger craft to dock with a space station. NASA got so many inquiries it had to post a note on its Web site saying the agency had nothing to do with the offer.

So what are all those would-be space travelers to do with that vacation money they didn't get to spend in space?

Well, how about a road trip in the walnut-lined, soundproofed cab of a custom Unimog equipped with a Blaupunkt stereo system, a six-CD carousel changer and computerized direction finder? It's going to have to do until something better comes along.

– February 23, 2001

Chapter 4

Money matters

Wall St. witchcraft:
A correction, shakedown or downturn?

My knowledge of the stock market is admittedly limited. I know you have to be a member to shop there, sort of like BJ's or Sam's Club.

But I have been fascinated by the arcane workings of "the market" since 1976. That's when I took a tip from an insider and bought a penny stock called McDonald Micradata, which immediately plummeted on the news of my purchase.

My first thought was that this was a concidence. But then the same thing happened the next four times that I bought stocks. I didn't get angry.

But I couldn't help wondering how they knew it was me?

The point is that they just know stuff that guys like me get headaches trying to figure out. They know how to read key economic indicators, like the consumer price index or the purchasing managers index. They know how to gauge the contractions and expansions in a wildly undulating market. They can even track the fluctuations in the "overnight Eurodollar" or break the money supply down into M1, M2 or M3.

Used to be that the rest of us didn't have to think about this stuff.

After all, it wasn't our money. Until we got smart enough to pull our money out of passbook savings accounts and learn how to pronounce "mutual fund."

page 77

And until the news of last week. But unless you have your handy economic glossary next to you when you read the paper, most of this is going over your head.

Until now. If you pay close attention, I will provide you with an axiom that helps you understand all you need to know about the ups and downs of a yo- yo market.

It's this simple: If it's good for you, it's bad for the whales on Wall Street, and vice versa.

Which is why yesterday's news that housing starts were down 11 percent was seen as a good sign by analysts. And things really took off when they learned that requests for building permits were off by 4 percent.

Of course, if you're looking to buy your dream house or if you work in the building trades, this is not good news to you. But you'll get over it.

The unemployment figures are another example. If they sink too low, investors get worried. Too many new people with jobs is a bad thing, even if most of those new jobs involve a spatula or spaghetti mop.

(You starting to sense a trend?)

Don't get me wrong. It's not that our friends in the investment community don't want us to do well, just not too well.

Because tight labor markets and high consumer spending tend to overheat the economy. And an overheated economy invites the intervention of Alan Greenspan, who can do more to make the market fluctuate than an earthquake on Wall Street.

Greenspan runs the Federal Reserve Bank. "The Fed," which is a quasi-public consortium of bankers who set interest rates and monetary policy, convenes eight times a year.

Nobody knows exactly who they are. But they get together behind closed doors in something called the Federal Open Market Committee, a phrase as false as "independent congressional investigation." Their meetings are so secret they make the College of Cardinals look like a chat room.

page 78

Next get-together is scheduled for May 16, when they will either raise interest rates or not, depending on how many jobs we have or houses we build. Apparently we have been working too hard and buying too much for our own good because the Fed has raised interest rates in almost every meeting for the last two years.

The effect is to tighten the money supply, making it hard for us to borrow for these spending sprees we've been on.

Tight money may be the one thing that works the same for us and the whales on Wall Street. You can tell this because the approach of the Federal Open Market Committee's deliberations sets off a feeding frenzy in the market. Whales wait for the panic, then scarf up bargains when small investors sell off their holdings.

Big investors can lose billions on paper, but they don't panic because they know the market is just right-sizing.

It's called a "correction," which is another name for a "shakeout," which is not to be mistaken for a "downturn."

I could explain all that. But let's face it: Most of us still wouldn't know a convertible debenture from a Chevy coupe.

– April 19, 2000

Some tax brackets creep the wrong way

If middle is a class, I'm in it. In fact, I'm all up in the middle of it judging by the most commonly held notions of what middle class is.

When I got into this business as a reporter for the Bulletin, I was working class. I don't remember what I made. I know the hourly rate was less than the $5 an hour they paid me as a part-timer. And, as we've all heard our fathers say, I was glad to get it.

But now, I have bracket-crept my way into the middle class, I think. I know I haven't reached upper middle class. I don't have the right toys for that. That's a class defined by its leisure. They vacation every few months in places bordered by beaches, mountains or both.

This class includes many people previously thought to be rich. There are upper-middle-class people with vacation homes hanging off cliffs that overlook ocean vistas - some have one on each coast. Some of them have combined family incomes in excess of $1 million per year. They differ from the rich mainly in that work is more than a hobby with them.

I know you hear about the other two main classes all the time. But just to review, they are the rich and the poor. And, oh, yeah, there's this new class called the working poor. These people run for their lives but never escape poverty. This used to be a substratum of the working class. But now more than 14 million of them work full-time jobs in America and still can't rise above the poverty level. They don't all flip burgers or use pointed sticks to stab candy wrappers in public parks.

page 80

In fact, the most dramatic change in the American economic scene today is that many of them hold what many of us once called "good jobs." For instance, there are cops in Philadelphia collecting food stamps to supplement the $23,000 we pay them to risk their lives.

Over the next few months most of the economic news out of Washington is going to be about tax breaks. Right now, Democrats and Republicans alike are falling over each other in a rush to give us a break.

I'm all for it. We could use a break.

But I can't help looking over my shoulder at the plight of the working poor. What's happening to them scares me.

They have become what no working American is ever supposed to be – downwardly mobile.

Because at the same time that the rich are blowing the roof off the economy, the floor is dropping out from under a lot of Americans who work every day.

And there is nothing out there for them. They don't have enough votes to attract special attention from tax reformers.

They're not quite poor enough to get in on the reforms the politicians say are in the works for the truly poor. And even though the few hundred dollars they get back from the tax break will help, it won't get them out of poverty.

In fact, the way the breaks are parceled out in this expanding economy, the working poor may soon be locked in mortal battle with the truly poor for the few crumbs the rest of us don't get.

I predict it won't come to that. What's more likely is that the politicians will soon realize how unfair it would be to create programs to help the truly poor get off welfare without extending those programs to the working poor, too.

My prediction is that they'll solve that problem by doing nothing for either of them.

Just suppose they decided to reform welfare in a way that would enable people to literally work their way off of public assistance. In order to get them jobs that didn't keep them forever on the brink of welfare eligibility, we'd have to provide some job training. Furthermore, you couldn't expect many welfare mothers to become working mothers without providing day care.

We still haven't gotten to the big-ticket item: health care.

A mother who gave up her medical-assistance card to become one of millions of working Americans who can't afford health insurance probably ain't smart enough to get much of a job anyway.

We could let them work and keep their medical assistance. But then, what do we say to the millions of working poor who have no protection at all?

Last year this time, there was still talk about "comprehensive health-care reform," which may have made it possible for every working American to afford health insurance. Maybe not.

The cost was prohibitive and there was a little hitch that made it a hard sell for the American public: Those of us who provide most of the votes already have health insurance and aren't that anxious to pay for other people's.

But it looks like we will get a tax break. The president wants to give us $30 billion to $40 billion over the next five years.

Republicans would give us $300 billion, a third of it in capital-gains-tax cuts.

I can't tell you what that comes to per person. For folks at the top of the eligibility list, it may be just enough for lawn darts.

It won't get the rest of us anywhere near one of those cliff houses overlooking the Atlantic or inside a Jag convertible. It's not going to be enough to change anybody's life, really.

Fortunately, most of us don't need our lives changed that much.

But it looks like another off-year for those who have neither pot nor window.

– *December 14, 1994*

Uniquely qualified to sort out bank mergers

My banking career ended abruptly when I was, ahhh, let go due to a chronic inability to arrive for work at the start of my shift. Banks are funny about that.

Before that, though, I literally handled hundreds of thousands of transactions each week at the First Pennsylvania Banking and Trust's operations center in the 3000 block of Market Street. The midnight mail crew sorted, on average, 10 or 12 sacks of mail an hour, a heavier volume than the town of Clifton Heights, our supervisor often bragged.

So, I am uniquely qualified to offer insights into the imminent merger of First Union and CoreStates banks. Unlike most reporters, whose banking experience is limited to sprinting to a branch office just ahead of their bouncing checks, I used to be a banker.

But even my eyes glazed over yesterday while the Daily News editorial board met with John Georgius, vice chairman of First Union. He talks about billions of dollars like it's lunch money.

Back in '75, he told us, First Union had a paltry $2 billion in assets and only earned a measly $10 million or so per annum. Today, they're worth $200 billion and earn about $4 billion a year. Little of this growth results from what you might call the walk-up trade.

First Union grew by swallowing smaller banks like Goobers. Georgius estimated that he has been personally involved in about 140 mergers and takeovers in his 23 years with First Union. Judging by the monograms on his cuff, I'd say he's banked a buck or two in his personal accounts.

His boss, Edward "Fast Eddie" Crutchfield, the CEO of First Union, ``earned" $19.5 million in personal compensation last year, a year in which a few thousand people became former employees. By the time they finish digesting CoreStates, hundreds more will join them in unemployment lines.

It's not hard to hate these people and their big bank. Reporters love to kick a guy when he's up.

But as tantalizing a target as First Union is, I'm willing to hold fire on this one for a couple of reasons. First of all, the wave of corporate combinations and mega-mergers that created this colossus is not a force of nature but a political climate that some of us helped create by electing the people we did.

The wave of corporate combinations and mega-mergers that created this colossus is not a force of nature but a political climate that some of us helped create by electing the people we did.

Banking deregulation swept through Congress almost unimpeded. Even after the trillion-dollar savings and loan fiasco, the American public was not alarmed enough to force a second look at the policies that unleashed this ravenous beast.

Besides, I'm not so sure that we're not better off with the financial options that these huge institutions are able to offer in what Georgius called their ``varied product lines."

The other thing that gives me pause is that people in the industry feel that the community banks which still serve the smallest depositors and businesses may actually benefit from these mergers. The banks that have been eaten up by these mergers were already too large to lose any sleep over.

We're not talking about Bob's Bank and Trust here.

Georgius painted a picture of a future just five years hence when there may be only five to 10 huge financial institutions. The 9,000 to 10,000 community banks will be culled and combined until there are, maybe, 6,000 to 7,000 left. Banks in the $30 billion to $40 billion range, like the one I was suddenly separated from, may cease to exist.

page 84

Emma Chappell, CEO of United Bank of Philadelphia, concurred.

"They were predicting this back when I was in graduate school in '82," she said. ``There will only be two kinds of banks, community banks and these megabanks or money centers.

"But for community banks like United, this environment is a great opportunity. There will always be depositors and small businessmen who want to talk to people in their own communities.

"We have to create strategic alliances that allow us to move our services closer to that public. We have formed one with Rite Aid to put our ATMs in 30 stores. We have put five others in police stations, where people can use them at no charge and feel safe."

So, you see, those of us with banking experience on the professional level aren't about to get our pinstripes twisted over this. When you've been around banking as long as I have, you learn to anticipate the trends.

– April 17, 1998

The rich inspire some idle thoughts

First thing you notice in the world of big-time sports is the vast number and wide variety of the really rich.

The most fun to watch are the ones who jab or dribble their way out of poverty and into incredible wealth. Some of these guys are into the kind of in-yo-face spending you or I might do if we became suddenly wealthy.

I remember watching Mike Tyson leave a post-fight party in one of his Lamborghini trucks the night he put Frank Bruno to sleep. He looked as if he were doing wheelies in a warthog.

Somebody said it cost more than $100,000 and that most are sold to the children of Arab oil millionaires who like to race through the desert at 100 miles an hour.

Tyson had two of these monster trucks, along with a fleet of luxury cars. There are ballplayers who decide which luxury car to drive by the color of the outfits they're wearing that night.

These guys spend more money on lug nuts than most of us spend on transportation altogether.

But I'm not just talking about athletes. The really rich are the ones who pay them.

I'm talking about guys like Jeffrey Lurie.

These are people who can spend $185 million and never say, "We'll have to tighten our belts a little, dear, but I think we can do it."

page 86

I don't know much about Mr. Lurie, but I'll bet he won't be running around the mansion shutting off the lights or looking for loose change under the sofa cushions to make this deal work.

This is a man who almost had to wrestle Norman Braman to the ground and stuff million-dollar bills in his pockets. And he still had to ward off suitors such as Ron Jaworski, who reportedly tried to get the Eagles for a measly $160 million last year.

We may quibble over the price. But Lurie thought it was fair. And anybody who thinks $185 million is a fair price for anything is somebody we're interested in.

That's why it caused such a stir when we heard that Lurie was going to sell his place in Beverly Hills and move to Philadelphia.

First off, anybody who would willingly trade a 902 ZIP code for a 191 bears watching. That's a fascinating move to people like us who have to live in the shadow of the groundhog.

But I think what really fascinates us about having the obscenely wealthy living nearby is that it allows us to become familiar with this alien breed.

We'll be calling him Jeff by the end of the week. Talk-show listeners will be calling in to tell Jeff how to spend his money.

It's a familiarity that can only breed contempt. Just ask Norm.

That's why we don't see a lot of really rich people in the steam line at Horn and Hardart's or dropping off their kids at the tot lot.

The really rich in the Philadelphia area have cultivated anonymity as a lifestyle. Around here, we pass people driving Plymouth station wagons who sit astride family fortunes worth hundreds of millions.

That's how you do it when you have old money. Folks with old money turn up their noses at people who pay $185 million to play ball. They buy art.

But to those of us whose money barely gets old enough to last till next payday, buying athletes by the truckload seems to make more sense than blowing millions on a picture of sunflowers somebody painted a hundred years ago.

page 87

And the big-time sports world is literally overrun by our kind of rich guys. George Steinbrenner could fill the Waldorf Astoria with people who would buy him out tomorrow if he sounded as if he'd sell the Yankees.

Don King used to have more trouble finding fat fighters to feed to his overweight champions than he did lining up millionaires to back his fights.

This country is crawling with them.

America is freaky for the amount of wealth amassed in the hands of the really rich. Only thing more interesting than how rich they get is how they get rich.

There must be a thousand people within a short walk of Central Park who could buy it if it were for sale. Some earn millions inventing things like the machine that puts pleats in hairpins.

All right, I made that part up. But the thing is, there are all kinds of people with all kinds of money and we like to look at them.

We want to look at Jeff Lurie and maybe at a few of those stars who made millions appearing in some of those mediocre movies he's been making.

We want to hear him calling in to jaw with the morning guys on all-sports radio. We want to see him leaning on the counter at Pat's Steaks with Cheez Whiz dripping down his chin.

It may mean much more than football. We may be able to get this guy to adopt a school, or even the whole school system.

Maybe he could save the Navy Yard by getting his friends to come in and have their yachts refitted or whatever it is they do to their yachts from time to time.

For now, though, we'll be satisfied if he can buy us one of those Super Bowls. A guy with that kind of money ought to be able to lure Jimmy Johnson out of retirement or buy us an Emmitt Smith.

What we know for sure is that success is for sale in the world of big-time sports.

This may be the man who can buy it for us.

– April 8, 1994

page 88

Lotto dreamin':
Well, first I'd...

By now, you have probably heard that I did not win the Big Game Lottery in New Jersey last night.

Like many of you, I did not match any of the six numbers on the bobbing ping pong balls that were drawn by a certified public accountant from a Big Four accounting firm at a secret ceremony staged in the official lottery cave, deep in the bowels of one of the six participating states.

But unlike most other no-fers, I didn't actually buy a ticket, which decreased my chance of winning only slightly. Besides, not having a ticket did not keep me out of the game because lottery mania is not about winning so much as about an excuse to indulge yourself in the most outlandish dreams you can conjure up.

And I don't need a ticket to dream.

I'm always coming up with novel ways to spend tens of millions of dollars. I do this because you never know when that next windfall may come.

And nothing is more embarrassing than not having an answer ready when a reporter asks what you're going to do with all that money.

It's such a simple question. You're not being asked for an econometric projection. You don't have to solve for X.

The answer should take this form: "Soon as you get these lights out of my face, I'm going out to buy the biggest..."

page 89

Yet you see it all the time. Some poor schlub who still has his milk money from kindergarten pinned to his mittens finally hits the biggie. He and the missus stand ramrod stiff in their best American Gothic pose as photographers jockey for position and reporters shout questions.

Somehow, this surprise question stumps them. We haven't had a chance to think about it yet, he says in all sincerity.

Haven't had a chance to think about it?

What was this doofus doing while the rest of us built dream castles and spent our imaginary dollars as if they had expiration dates on them?

This thing has been going on for more than four months. That's how long it's been since anybody won one of these weekly Big Game lotteries.

Next time someone who has spent the last 43 years screwing lug nuts into passing cars on an auto assembly line says he's not sure he will quit his job, I will personally confiscate his ticket.

Anybody who can't come up with a dream in that many weeks should be disqualified. They probably found the winning ticket when they bent over to pick up a penny.

And the dream-challenged aren't the only ones whose tickets should be confiscated. They ought to disqualify anybody who would win $325 million, then fix his or her face to say that they aren't sure whether they will quit working.

Next time someone who has spent the last 43 years screwing lug nuts into passing cars on an auto assembly line says he's not sure he will quit his job, I will personally confiscate his ticket.

Let me be real clear on this, boss. I love what I do. But I'd be like Abraham, Martin and John if I hit the big one. You'd just look around, and I'd be gone.

Not that I'd be content to let my meat loaf. After a long, slow broil on some distant beach, when I was sure I was well done on both sides, I'd be ready to pursue one of the business opportunities my new wealth would open to me.

page 90

And the more I think about it, what would make the most sense would be to get into a game like the one I had just won.

Because the lottery is a license to print money. Where else can you offer people a tiny chance to win and expect them to raise their bets as you raise the odds against winning?

By my own semi-scientific calculations, you are more likely to be bitten by a snaggle-toothed barracuda on Broad Street than to find yourself pondering the choice between the $125-million instant cash-out or the $10-million-a-year-for-26-years option.

With those kinds of odds working for them, it's not hard to figure why the states hoard this action for themselves and arrest anyone who tries to compete.

But with that $325 million from last night's lottery tucked in my jeans, I could have bought a small state and set up my own game. Or I could have found that one drop of Iroquois blood coursing through my veins and opened an Indian casino in Wildwood. They've been looking for a tribe to get them in the game for a long time down there.

– May 10, 2000

Legalized gambling: The sky's the limit

Thing that used to amaze me most about Las Vegas was the number of permanent residents who thought they were just passing through.

There were people who had missed the bus back to L.A. five or six years earlier but still figured they'd get "home" some day if they could just turn up the right card or make the dice land on the right number. I couldn't bring myself to tell them that the old lady had stopped warming up their dinner a few summers ago. 'Cause hey, their luck could change any minute for all I knew.

What I'm getting to here is that, for years, I have allowed this sort of thing to turn me off to casino gambling as a possible source of revenue for overtaxed, underserviced Philadelphians. For too long now, the plight of the pitiful few has blinded me to benefits gambling offers the larger population.

Reviewing the three complete columns and a dozen dishonorable mentions devoted to the subject since 1992, I'm afraid I have not been entirely fair to the dedicated men and women in sleeve garters who redistribute our wealth in casinos and riverboats all over America. More recent research shows that whole towns have been yanked back from the brink of oblivion by gaming revenues.

A case in point is East St. Louis, Ill. I was there in 1992, shortly after an impatient businessman walked into city hall and repossessed Mayor Gordon Bush's typewriter.

Turns out that this was not the low point for the city hall staff. They had already learned to either bring toilet paper from home or just hold it. After you endure a few payless paydays, you learn not to sweat the small stuff.

Mayor Bush had earned a reputation for resourcefulness by working out a settlement with a family who actually owned city hall, having won it in a lawsuit filed on behalf of a loved one whose head was caved in by a cellmate in an unsupervised city lockup.

I found Bush surprisingly upbeat for the mayor of a town that had not had regular trash collection in seven years and smelled like it.

He walked me to the window of his spacious but sparsely furnished office and pointed to a parcel of riverfront property which was to be the site of East St. Louis' future. His eyes filled up as he began to describe the $5 million in annual revenue and the 250 permanent jobs for local residents that he anticipated.

The big boat that saved East St. Louis is called the Casino Queen. It's been pouring about $6 million a year into the city treasury.

"You should see [East St. Louis] now," said Fred Faust, a reporter who covers the gaming industry for the St. Louis Post-Dispatch.

"All the police cars have radios. The trash gets picked up all the time. You remember how sad it was a few years ago. Well, it's making quite a comeback."

Some Missourians do not share Fred Faust's warm feeling for their neighbor across the river. Seems their own year-old entry into the floating casino industry hasn't fared well in the competition with East St. Louis for the region's disposable income. "The Casino Queen took a little hit when the 'Admiral' first opened on the Missouri side of the river," Faust said. "But the revenues have been a little disappointing on this side."

Faust speculated that better parking on the Illinois side of the river is why the Casino Queen outdraws the Admiral. But I think not.

page 93

I think the difference is that Missouri allows patrons to lose only up to $500 a day while Illinois permits limitless losing. The term "man overboard" has real meaning on an Illinois riverboat.

Which brings me back to our own river and Mayor [Ed] Rendell's dream of new revenues from casino gambling.

As the example of East St. Louis shows us too clearly, if you want to make big money, you have to take the shackles off people and let 'em bet it all.

Missouri wasn't the first state to lose its shirt on gambling moderation when Illinois got in the game.

Iowa raked in $7.3 million in taxes and $1.9 million for the state's gambler's assistance fund from its five floating casinos when they first opened in 1991.

The next year, Illinois got into the game with its "sky's-the-limit" gambling. Casinos popped up on 15 Indian reservations in and around Iowa, and things just weren't the same.

In fact, two of Iowa's five boats pulled up anchor and sailed south to Mississippi where gambling is so unregulated they'll let you run a riverboat on a puddle as long as you're not a card-carrying mafioso.

That's what we're going to have to do here if we want our big wheel to keep on turning. How long do you think it will take New Jersey to open its floating craps game if we start running casino boats on our side of the river?

And then there's New York City. They're already losing money to Atlantic City and on Indian reservations in Connecticut. How long can we expect them to stand pat with a losing hand?

Our only choice is to get in big and get in early. And forget about those regulations. Let 'em lose it all for the greater good. You might be surprised how many new people may settle here on their way through town.

— *April 12, 1995*

page 94

Church keeps rein
on money managers

I didn't just flunk economics. I had to be led from class by security personnel for fear I'd trip over a theorem and hurt myself.

My wife, a business education and accounting major, handles all household accounts. I may be the only professional in this building who has neither a MAC card nor a checking account.

And this is fine with me. It gets me out of paperwork and reduces the risk that I'll put my eye out with a No. 2 pencil.

Despite this, I was elected to the trustee board of my church, where I'm allowed to count money as long as I'm surrounded by people who can talk me through it and make sure I'm not a danger to myself or others.

It is through these people that I learned something about fiscal security. The Tabernacle Baptist Church can't buy a communion wafer without the signature of three senior trustees.

So I'm trying to figure out how a guy named Nick Leeson who is not as old as an average British banker's cravat can mess up enough money to bankrupt a 233-year-old financial institution. We're not talking about Honest Bob's bank and trust. This is (or was before the Dutch firm ING bought it for $1.60 billion) Barings PLC, London.

Barings is the bank that checked Thomas Jefferson's figures before backing the Louisiana Purchase. They financed the Napoleonic Wars.

page 95

Nick Leeson is 28 years old, for God's sake, and not particularly mature for his age, judging from the fact that his idea of fun is to drop his pants in public.

Between moonshots, Leeson spent his time trading futures and options out of Barings' Singapore office. His officer job was to do settlements, which put him in the enviable position of making trades and accounting for them.

Hey, what with staffing cuts and all, a lot of us are pulling double duty. But this is not like some guy in Detroit doing headlights and taillights on the same car.

This is more like being an Earp and a Clanton at the same time.

How does this happen? Who do you have to know to get a job like this?

The financial community in general is waiting with bated breath for the answers to these and other questions about Leeson's Singapore swap meet.

The answers are expected forthwith, now that Leeson's vacation plans were interrupted abruptly by German police who pulled him and his wife from a plane in Frankfurt last week.

Leeson has promised to tell all he knows and more, not only about his own part in this scam but also about his silent partners back in the boardroom who, as they say at Academy Awards time, made it all possible.

And who can blame him for singing the Will Tell overture? They're threatening to try him in Singapore, where you can get 10 years and 40 lashes for spitting on the street. No telling what they'll do to a guy who blows a billion bucks of other people's money.

When the truth comes out, one thing they'll surely learn is that a lot of Leeson's bosses got whiplash looking the other way while he was doing his thing.

Usually, if somebody earns a million a month for you, you'd want him to say how. That way, if he calls in sick somebody else can work the levers. Otherwise, flu season could really wipe you out.

Unless you suspect something slightly slimy about the operation that's making you rich. Then you see and don't see.

page 96

All the veddy veddy British bankers who backed his play with huge sums of cash claim the only thing they knew about Leeson's derivatives trading is that it made millions and cost millions. So, as late as six weeks before the sky fell, Barings was borrowing part of the $850 million Leeson blew on Japanese stock market bets.

This was more money than the bank was worth, raising a question that won't get answered in Singapore: How is it that the same regulators who can keep you or me from getting a $100,000 mortgage on a $50,000 house can allow a bank to blow more than the total value of its assets on a bet?

The answer, in a word, is GREED. Back when it still paid to look the other way, they took the money in their back pockets without turning around to see where it came from.

Which may be how a Democratic county treasurer named Robert Citron could bankrupt a county full of rich Republicans in the billion-dollar Orange County debacle last year.

Of course nobody knows how that happened either, or how money managers in a half-dozen towns, school districts and major corporations have managed to override their oversights and lose billions in markets they now say they didn't understand.

All they know is that they zigged when they should have zagged or bobbed when they should have weaved. Next thing they knew, the money was gone.

So, I'm sitting here thinking about how somebody could even fix his face to say something like this to the trustees and congregation of the Tabernacle Baptist Church.

Fortunately, we never need to worry about that. Our Bible teaches us to "Watch as well as pray."

– *March 8, 1995*

page 97

Why do we get the tab? Because the poor can't pay it and the rich won't

After an exhaustive study of data culled from authoritative sources, it is finally clear to me why the bulk of the tax burden falls so disproportionately on the American middle.

It's because that's where we are.

By we, I mean the people in two distinct categories – everybody who is either reading or writing this column.

Us.

We get to bear the bulk of the burden because everybody else is either too poor to pay attention or too rich to be bothered.

Which only leaves those of us who are in the middle.

But it's not really the middle, except that we're midway between the proverbial rock and a hard place.

To think of that vast category between abject poverty and fabulous wealth as the "middle" makes it sound like there are roughly as many of them as there are of us.

Actually, nothing could be farther from the truth.

Under the revised tax code, middle income includes everybody who earned between damned near nothing and a whole buncha money.

The rule of thumb is that if you don't sleep in the street or own one, you are part of the we who provide the money which makes America work.

page 98

Seeing it that way takes a lot of the pressure off us. We no longer have to worry about the once-dreaded "bracket creep." It's no longer a sliding scale.

The top is too high to reach and the bottom too low to stoop just to duck a tax bill.

So we should bear our burdens cheerfully, secure in the knowledge that this really is our country because we paid for it.

I raise all of this only because of the unseemly grousing that is starting to be heard from the middle.

There are those who feel we should be getting more help from above.

Not the "above" most of us look to when our burdens get heavy – just a bracket or two above, where the wealthy frolic freely in their tax shelters.

The moans from the middle have gotten so loud it's disturbing deliberations in Washington where our elected officials have huddled to total our tax bills.

As if they didn't have enough to think about already – with issues like sequestration and reelection – here comes all this weeping and wailing from America's whining we.

"We're already paying for war and peace and crime and punishment," we whine.

"What do they want from us now, the salt from our shakers? the paper from our walls?"

It's a pitiful sight, all this whimpering and whining – and from the people America counts on most.

As President Bush keeps reminding us, there is nobody better suited to pay than we.

The poor can't and the rich won't.

Fact is, Mr. Bush informs us, the rich really shouldn't be expected to pay any more taxes.

Which is why Bush doesn't want their bubbles busted or their rates raised.

Busting their bubbles would mean that families who earn more than $217,000 per year would have to pay a top rate of 33 percent, just like people in the bracket just below them.

The present tax code allows them to pay preferred or "bubble" top rate of 28 percent, which leaves them a little to put aside for campaign contributions.

page 99

The president and loyalist Republicans say the best way the government can get more money from the rich is to cut their capital gains taxes.

This would encourage the truly rich to sell off some of those palatial mansions and other fabulous doodads they've been amassing in their bubbles.

Turns out these things don't bring the wealthy that much joy.

They've only been holding them until the time when we can get the best advantage from their sale.

As soon as we get the capital gains rate down from 28 percent to 15 percent, the truly rich can finally begin their five-car garage sale.

The taxes from that big asset sell-off should be enough to bring our boys back home from the sands of Saudi Arabia and the shelters of our major cities.

– October 18, 1990

Suit up political players; party lines too blurred

Switching back and forth from ``Monday Night Football" to the Republican National Convention, I could see what it would take to restore meaning to our two-party system.

Uniforms.

I can't tell you how many guys riding with the Cowboys this year hauled muskets for the Patriots in past years or vice versa. But with the emancipation proclamation of free agency permitting players to sell their services to the highest bidder, there's a comfort in the color-coding system.

Watching Pat Buchanan embracing Bob Dole who was embracing Jack Kemp who was embracing whatever principle du jour the party served up as the blue-plate special, makes you realize that in politics, you can't know the players even with a program.

But that's all right with me. Back when I thought I knew who they were, the Republicans weren't much fun for me to watch.

In Houston, when Buchanan declared, ``my friends, we must take back our cities, and take back our culture and take back our country," it was kind of scary.

I wasn't sure who he had declared Holy War on. I just knew I wasn't in the group he called ``my friends."

But watching the Republicans this year is like watching the Democrats.

This year, Republicans can be for or against almost anything and never have to worry about being hauled up before the membership committee.

page 101

As a person who is neither Democrat nor Republican but nonetheless very political, it's gratifying to see the two-party system melt down into a formless mass of ideological goop. It was one thing to choose sides when guys like Barry Goldwater and Hubert Humphrey duked it out for our hearts and minds. Back then it meant something to be a Democrat or a Republican or a liberal or conservative.

But you couldn't even pitch a small tent in the ideological territory that separates Bob Dole from Bill Clinton. On any given day, they can be found to the right or left of each other, depending on where they think we are.

No, they're not the same. And if I had to choose today, I'd cast a reluctant vote for Clinton, mainly because the stock market hasn't crashed, the world is not at war and Democrats don't hate cities or brown-skinned immigrants quite as much as Republicans do.

As far as party ideology is concerned, Democrats and Republicans seem poles apart on affirmative action and reproductive rights. When you look closer, though, you see that most Republicans agree with most Democrats on both of those issues.

The difference between Bill "The Compromiser" Clinton and Bob "The Dealmaker" Dole is largely about emphasis. And the American people know it.

That's why all the flapdoodle about pro-choice vs. pro-life, Christian coalitions vs. moderate pragmatists, etc., will have little or no effect on the outcome of this presidential election, just as they had little effect on the last one and will have little on the next one.

Affirmative action is a live issue. But it's more divisive than defining. The top of the Republican ticket is a case in point. Kemp claims he's for it, although he is now making noises against it. Dole voted boldly for it when he was in Congress but apparently opposes it as a presidential nominee.

Which means neither is willing to provide any leadership, so both will do whatever they think you want.

page 102

There is not a single issue in America, not even a combination of two or three issues, which can turn this election one way or another. Most of us won't vote at all and the ones who do will pick the man they think will do the least to upset things.

It's not about the rich. They might outspend us but they sure can't outvote us.

It's not about the poor. Despite the rhetoric, they know that neither party or presidential candidate is for them.

The rest of us can claim to be shocked that Bill Clinton would sign a welfare bill that may plunge a million children into poverty.

But the poor heard him four years ago when he said he'd change welfare as we know it.

They knew what that meant; so did we.

We know what it means when Bob Dole takes a giant step to the left to meet Jack Kemp, who took a giant step to the right to meet him, and when Colin Powell steps back to keep from getting crushed in the middle by his party's homogenized standard bearers. It means next to nothing in your life or mine and that's just the way we like it.

In a couple of weeks the Democratic glee club will meet to sing ``That's What America Is to Me.'' Then the red, white and blue balloons will drop on Bill Clinton and Al Gore.

A week later the NFL season will open. And, for a change, we'll be able to tell one side from another at a glance.

– August 14, 1996

page 103

Chapter 5

Little ones

Let's give it a try – and keep eye on kids

We're all sitting in the family room doing our separate things. My granddaughter Ashley, then 6, is transfixed by whatever is on the TV screen.

This is right after dinner. It's not quite dark out when the inane patter on some sitcom produces this riveting dialogue.

She: "Oh, yeah?"

He: "Yeah!"

She: "Oh, yeah?"

He: "Yeah!"

She: "Well, if you do, you'll be having sex alone."

To which my granddaughter replies, "That's dumb. You can't have sex alone."

The rest of us kind of glanced up from our reading without saying anything to each other. And since she wasn't talking to anyone in particular, none of us said anything to Ashley either.

My wife and I, having no doubt mishandled this sensitive area 20 years earlier when our daughter was that age, were just glad we didn't have to deal with it. My daughter, apparently taking the "less-said-the-better" tack, let the moment pass without comment. We're not sure where Ashley learned that sex was not a solo pursuit or, for that matter, what else she has heard on the subject. But we were certain that this signaled the need for a closer scrutiny of what she watches on TV.

page 107

It prompted us to shoo her away from the TV on Sunday evenings when ``Married with Children" comes on. Much of that show's comedic content is so loaded with sexual innuendo it's embarrassing to watch with small children. The interplay between the Bundy siblings features repeated references to her sexual promiscuity and his affinity for latex lovers.

Aside from being stupid and stereotypical, it's harmless fun for most of the family. But I wouldn't want to be a parent trying to explain to a small child what Bud Bundy does with rubber women.

And this, mind you, is on during the family hour. Which may be why parents groups and others have pressured the president to do something about the unfettered flow of sex and violence into living rooms. And although the First Amendment is my favorite piece of legislation, I'm with them.

At least, I'm with them up to a point. I'm against prohibiting sexual content or violence. I get antsy when people try to dictate what the rest of us can see or hear.

But I also don't have a lot of patience with First Amendment zealots who throw a tantrum every time someone suggests that labeling TV shows or movies or records is a good way to help parents make decision about what their children see or hear.

Labeling and rating systems are not a threat to the American way of life. They are not the same as book burnings, and they do not deny us our God-given right to bestiality or dismemberings or whatever else we want to watch.

I'm not so sure the TV rating system that the industry borrowed from Jack Valenti, the creator of the movie rating system, is much use. It was formally announced yesterday and will go into use as early as next month.

But unlike a lot of commentators on either side of this issue, I'm willing to give it a shot until something better comes along.

The most common complaint is that it doesn't offer enough information about the content of specific shows, instead offering a label on the general content of a series.

page 108

Naturally there are a few dead zones between the borders of these new categories. For instance, I don't know which category to place a recent episode of ``Nature,'' which showed a sex-starved bull elephant pressing his affections on a young female.

And should a young viewer be protected from the wanton violence of a pack of hyenas in a feeding frenzy tearing the flesh from a still-writhing African antelope?

I don't know. Some parents find ``Bambi'' too traumatic for their youngsters; others have no problem with sitting their children in front of graphic depictions of mob violence.

But when the menu is so broad and parents are so diverse in their views, what's wrong with offering them a little guidance in making their choices?

If the existence of ratings has a chilling effect on TV producers and causes them to turn out less sex and violence than they might otherwise, that ain't censorship. It's the free market at work.

They spend millions on research to find out what we want to watch.

This won't cost them or us a penny.

– December 20, 1996

page 109

Our little ones are getting a raw deal

Ashley usually runs into my bedroom with her little morning report just about the time her mother is racing to leave for work and drop her off at nursery school.

But you can't rush her. Whatever she has to say is always too important to just blurt out.

Yesterday it was a question.

"Um, um, Pop-Pop," she says breathlessly, "if I go to that school you can pick me up after you leave your work? Right, Pop-Pop?

"You can just go to work and sign your name and come and get me? Right, Pop-Pop?"

"Right, sweetheart," I tell her. "Pop-Pop will come and get you."

I really don't know what she's talking about - I think it's something about some school her mother wants to enroll her in.

Doesn't matter.

All she really wants to know is that I will be there for her when she needs me, that she can count on me to make it all right.

For some reason, only four years into a life that has been remarkably free of trauma, Ashley feels the need to line up her loved ones every so often.

But that's OK. Because only four years into grandfatherhood, it still feels good to have a child counting on me again.

She makes me feel my worth, lets me know why I'm here.

On the drive to work, I hear Billy Joel singing his beautiful lullaby "Good Night My Angel." And in the hushed, almost reverent, tones of this sweet assurance, I hear him feeling the same thing.

But then, seemingly in the next moment, another feeling breaks through.

I'm at my desk looking at a news photo of five small caskets lining the front of an auditorium being viewed by an anguished mother limp with grief and by a choir of children who must suddenly cope with the rough reality that we can't always make it all right.

The story says these five beautiful children were found huddled together in the ashes of a bathroom where they died, probably still believing until the very last that someone they counted on would come for them.

Please don't read this as an indictment or an accusation of anyone in those children's chain of care. By all accounts they were well-kept and as well-loved as my granddaughter or Joel's child.

It's just that losing them and the five other children who perished in house fires over the last few days in this area makes us feel helpless in the face of forces that don't respect our stewardship of these angels in our care.

But what frustrates me is that we are more and more impotent in dealing with the issues and forces any society ought to be able to protect its children from.

A few months ago I sat in on a Black History Month essay contest at the School District administration building on the Parkway. Nine of the best and brightest elementary school children in the district shared their feelings about our past and their future.

Six of the first seven children recited speeches about the drugs and violence in their schools and neighborhoods. These were top students from good homes reciting speeches they had written themselves.

If these children were that concerned about drugs and violence, I didn't even want to think about how children in our least stable homes and crime-ridden neighborhoods are coping.

page 111

I didn't have to think about it yesterday. The numbers were laid out in yesterday's editions.

The fastest-growing category of chronically poor people in America is infants and toddlers, according to a report released yesterday by the Government Accounting Office.

The number of poor children under age 3 had risen by 26 percent from 1.8 million to 2.3 million in the last 10 years. One out of five infants and toddlers in America lives in poverty.

And for some unknown reason, in the face of this increased poverty, the GAO says that young children are less likely than ever to be reached by federal early-childhood programs. It cited as an example Head Start, the federal pre-school program, which serves only 1 percent of the poorest infants and toddlers.

The GAO report followed close on the heels of one issued late last week by the Carnegie Foundation which said that children under the age of 3 are "society's most neglected age group."

The Carnegie Foundation cited a statistic that I have heard before but have never been able to understand.

"Compared with most other industrialized countries," the report said, "the United States has a higher infant mortality rate, a higher proportion of low birth- weight babies and a smaller proportion of babies immunized against childhood diseases."

In other words, we're losing children every day to forces that are well within our ability to cope with. Nations we prop up with foreign aid somehow take better care of their newborn and soon-to-be-born children than we do.

For me, it's like talking to a man in a pressed suit and starched shirt who has children somewhere living in poverty. There's nothing he can tell me.

I can't respect a man who takes better care of himself than he does of his children.

You wonder if our children will soon lose respect for a society that does the same thing.

– *April 13, 1994*

page 112

Save the children from GOO

It was like flipping on a light switch in a dirty kitchen.

The new president of all the people proposed immunizing all American children and the gang from GOO scurried for the baseboards for fear his foot would come down on about a half a dozen of them.

GOO? GOO is the Government Office of Obfuscation. It's also just what it sounds like, a sticky mess where good ideas go to die.

It is to good but simple ideas what the LaBrea tar pits were to saber-toothed tigers. It is to well-meaning concepts what a black hole is to starlight. It's a roach motel where grand schemes go in but can't come out.

The gang from GOO are government confusion specialists. They function to make you think that simple solutions can't fit complex problems.

The way it works is that every time some well-meaning dufus from Duluth starts a sentence that says "How come you guys don't just . . , " GOO dispatches a leaning tower of babble with a Ph.D. in condescension to bury him in a blizzard of technical terms.

They say stuff like: "What you've got to understand is that there is a multiplicity of factors to be weighed, a broad array of constituencies to be accommodated, a veritable plethora of issues and individuals to be considered."

Or: "There is much in what you say. However if you were equipped with even a rudimentary understanding of the complex interrelation of these seemingly disparate functions you'd know that the synergistic . . ."

page 113

Dufus heads back to Duluth with all this mush marinating in his brain and the gang from GOO do a high-five and return to their pinochle game in the Pentagon basement.

Except this time instead of a dufus from Duluth they got a hick from Hope who happens to be the new president of all the people.

This guy's a real problem. He's been on the job just long enough that he still loves turning the knobs and working the levers.

Plus, he's so fluent in English he can keep the beat when they run their riffs. So when the new president of all the people proposes a simple solution the gang from GOO can't cross his eyes with the weight of their words.

That's why this immunization thing sent seismic shivers through the Pentagon basement. It just might work, jeopardizing the comfortable careers of a whole battalion of guys who get paid to study a thing to death.

In fact this very thing got studied into an early grave a few years back. Somebody passed a law in 1986 ordering the U.S. Department of Health and Human Services to develop a national plan to immunize children.

It almost got started a year later. Then somebody ordered a study and it got mired in GOO.

This is the idea they studied to death:

The federal government and the states get together and buy up all the vaccines for measles, mumps, whooping cough and other things kids get, and then give them the shots at cost.

Only about half the kids in America get these shots, maybe one in 10 in the poorest neighborhoods. The people who studied the problem concluded that this was one of the reasons so many of these same kids get measles, mumps, whooping cough and other diseases.

But somewhere between conception and execution, the idea disappeared from the radar screen. Until now.

Naturally, just as the mummy of the '86 immunization plan began unraveling, a new enemy popped up – the pharmaceutical firms.

page 114

They rose in righteous indignation to complain that the universal purchase of vaccines would keep them from doing all these wonderful things they were fixing to do for the kids.

If they have to sell all their bug juice to the government, an industry spokesman said, it will cut their profits and force them to slash spending for research on new and better vaccines.

"Universal purchase would just kill innovation," Thomas L. Copmann, a spokesman for the Pharmaceutical Manufacturers Association, told the New York Times.

In other words, parents, better you sacrifice the health of your kids today so they may be even healthier tomorrow.

You'd have to be dumber than peat moss to go for that line. But inner-city parents are, according to the Pharmaceutical Manufacturers Association.

In fact, they claim the real reason inner-city parents don't immunize their kids is not that they can't afford the $244 per child a full set of immunizations cost, but that they just don't know any better, poor devils.

Anyway, I'm rooting for the new president of all the people. I gave him my lukewarm support last year only because he wasn't the old president of all the people.

But I'm starting to warm up to the guy because I like the way he works the knobs.

This thing of his about just doing things may not be a phase; it could be a trend.

He might start to say things like, "If Head Start works for the kids we've provided it for, why not give it to the rest of them?" Or, "If it costs us less to defend ourselves against toy soldiers in places like Libya, Granada and Panama, why not spend a few of those defense dollars on teachers and books?"

What a concept. It could work too, if we can just keep him away from the Pentagon basement.

– *February 2, 1993*

Chapter 6

Ramona Africa (Jim MacMillan/Daily News)

Newsmakers

Being there:
Eyewitness to history

Nelson Mandela moves cautiously down the steps leading from his veranda to the front lawn of his private residence outside Johannesburg.

Despite his casual attire and halting gait, his bearing is as regal on this day in October 1996 as it had been six years earlier when the world watched him walk away from 27 years in prison and into the leadership of a morally bankrupt nation.

The madiba is 78. But his lanky frame is unbent by the yoke of leadership. His thick gray mane and deeply lined face make him appear more wise than old. He seems far more relaxed than we are.

We are 11 journalists from eight nations who have been granted an audience with one of the most admired men on earth. Among us, we have met many of the most revered and most reviled figures of our times.

But nothing has prepared us for this moment. There is one Mandela and we are with him.

We are asked not to take flash pictures because his eyes have been damaged by limestone dust during years of forced labor in the Robben Island Prison Camp. But his eyes reveal nothing of the sorrow and suffering he has surely endured.

That is a part of his history that Mandela does not allow himself or his nation to dwell on. He alone had the moral authority to sell South Africa's black majority on reconciliation instead of revenge. His ability to translate his own forbearance and forgiveness into national policy was direct pressure on an open wound.

page 119

Repressed resentments still simmer. Eruptions of ethnic violence and a startling upsurge in violent crime are ominous. But South Africa will survive its birthing pains because the transition from racist regime to representative republic was led by a man who would not be king.

A long-forgotten history lesson comes to mind as I recall that day. What made George Washington the father of his country? a teacher once asked. He was the father of his country, she told us, because he stepped aside when he could have been president for life. Like Mandela he was a figure of such heroic proportions that he could have overshadowed the birth of the republic.

Adulation is a powerful intoxicant. But Mandela and Washington understood that the strength of a new nation is in an orderly transfer of power. They understood what such great African revolutionaries as Jomo Kenyatta and Julius Nyerere didn't: You must trust your people even if they don't trust themselves.

They say history is written by the conquerers. Maybe. But it is recorded by people like the 11 journalists who stood in awe on Mandela's lawn.

Our eye witness accounts will be collected and culled long after were gone. Nothing about any of us will last except our testimony.

I THINK ABOUT IT a lot. I thought about it in a courtroom in Jackson, Mississippi where justice finally caught up with Byron Dela Beckwith. This tired, broken old man was but a shadow of the rabid racist who hid in the honeysuckle across from Evers' house and shot him in the back as he was sorting through his keys.

Beckwith sat silently as the only notable event in his otherwise insignificant life was retold in graphic testimony his back curved, his blue veins visible through transparent skin. I almost felt sorry for him.

But then I remembered the testimony and I could almost see this slithering snake in the honeysuckle, squinting through the sight of his Enfield rifle.

page 120

I remembered Myrlie Evers' testimony about how she and her children huddled inside as shots rang out, how they rushed outside and found their daddy clutching his keys in a puddle of blood. I remember her describing the children's frantic screams: "Daddy get up! Get up!"

And I knew that, while we must forgive, we can never forget.

I CAN NEVER FORGET the gulf between the perception of Russia I had been taught growing up in the Cold War years and the reality I saw when I went there in the aftermath of the Communist Party's collapse.

Good had triumphed over evil in a story line colored by our political overlay. The truth, I would discover, was much more nuanced than that jingoistic history.

Adulation is a powerful intoxicant. But Mandela and Washington understood that the strength of a new nation is in an orderly transfer of power. They understood what such great African revolutionaries as Jomo Kenyatta and Julius Nyerere didn't: You must trust your people even if they don't trust themselves.

I saw an oppressed people, struggling to reconcile the utter collapse of their way of life with a new world order in which they were no longer dominant. I saw a people who had endured, the humiliation of czarist serfdom, the mass murder of Stalinist purges and the brutal regimentation of Soviet-style Communism. They would stand, even when their leaders fell.

In Somalia I watched dying children with swollen bellies and vacant eyes and wondered how future generations would judge us. How do you explain what we called compassion fatigue or the idea that people saw the Somalis as unworthy of the same charity we were seeing lavished on refugees in Eastern Europe?

But the real story on the ground was of the heroic efforts of nameless people who put their own lives on hold in an extraordinary act of love. I saw doctors, nurses and relief teams risk their lives in a war zone to feed and starving children who didn't look like them. The story I told was not the one I went for.

Some day, some historian or social scientist will retrieve the automated files our history will be recorded on at that time.

I like to believe that they will find something I wrote and compare it to other accounts and to their own research.

The resulting composite will become the history of our times. It may be too much to expect. But not too much to prepare for.

Ramona Africa: After the fire

The burn scars run along Ramona Africa's forearms like stigmata embossed in the fabric of her flesh.

They have healed, but in a way that will leave her marked for as long as she lives. She is the survivor, the only adult who emerged from the flaming ruins of Osage Avenue and lived to talk about it.

The events of May 13, 1985, have been seared into her soul. And they are a part of a story that only she can tell as she carries MOVE's message around the world.

How she and the young boy known as Birdy Africa survived the fire that killed 11 MOVE members, including six children, are what people want her to talk about in the forums that her victim status have opened to her. And she will talk about it if you ask her.

I asked her where Birdy was. She shrugged. "Last I heard," she said, "he was in Germany. His father talked him into joining the Army."

I didn't ask much about that day when I met her at the American Friends Service Committee at 15th and Cherry. She called to say she would talk on the 15th anniversary of the fire if I wanted to.

But the fire is not what MOVE members talk about in their international speaking tour. They have spoken to Parliament members in England, to the German Reischstag, to students and activists all over Europe and United States.

page 123

But once she has their attention, she shifts to the only topics that matters to her now, the fate of the nine MOVE members who have spent the last 21 years in jail for the shooting death of Patrolman James Ramp on August 8, 1979, and Mumia Abu-Jamal.

"They ask about what happened on May 13," she said. "They want to know what happened and why it happened.

"But they certainly don't focus on the gruesome details ... What purpose would that serve?

"People know that this city dropped a bomb on our family, including babies.

"A lot of people don't focus on the fact that there were bullet fragments found in the bodies. Our family wasn't allowed to escape the fire.

"People want to know why I went to jail . . . I tell them I went to jail because I survived the massacre."

They covered survival in the criminal code under the charge of felony riot. I may be able to rationalize the charge, but the sentence still seems unjust.

She was sentenced to 16 months to seven years. She served the maximum because she refused to renounce MOVE.

"This was not like telling a criminal he can't associate with known felons." she said. "Has the MOVE organization ever been declared a criminal organization?

"Do they tell Muslims or Christians not to associate with their people?

". . . I have never regretted it. That's a real easy decision for MOVE people . . . John Africa has taught us that this system can't offer us freedom."

But freedom is what she seeks in her transcontinental evangelism, freedom for the MOVE nine and Abu-Jamal.

It's a message that resonates more as she gets farther from this city. In this town, we're mostly tired of hearing about it, tired of reliving the pain.

"I can understand that," she concedes. "In Philadelphia there are people who bear a lot of guilt.

"It's always easier to deal with something far away. People here could deal with the injustice of apartheid because it was far away.

page 124

". . . But racism is a disease no matter where or who it comes from. Didn't black people acquit Wilson Goode?"

She talks, almost matter-of-factly about running into former Mayor Wilson Goode in the post office a few years ago.

"He saw me and turned to talk to this little boy," she recalled. "I didn't confront him. I confronted him in court."

Confrontations are rare these days with MOVE. They live in peace with their neighbors near 45th Street and Kingsessing Avenue in Southwest Philadelphia.

But, they haven't mellowed, she says.

"Maybe it's the neighbors who have changed, not MOVE," she says slyly.

"We will never stop fighting for our family. But we don't shout now because people hear what we're saying.

Maybe. Or maybe they have finally learned that more people were turning off than tuning in to their rants.

For me, it was just good to hear from her and to be reminded that someone survived the flames of May 13, 1985.

– May 12, 2000

No answer at roll call:
It was the trying that defined Hank Gather's life

I was never the same after the death of Robert Brown.

You wouldn't have known him. He didn't live long enough to do very much. He was just this chubby dude I met in 7th grade at Shoemaker Junior High School.

Most of us liked him a lot. He liked to laugh and make us laugh. But he was gone by the time we got to 8th grade.

One morning they called roll and he didn't answer. We learned he had been in an automobile accident, and eventually understood that he was dead.

It was that understanding that changed me. I liked him. But to be honest, his death had a greater impact on me than his life had.

His wasn't the first death I had experienced.

In 1954, my Uncle Grover died in a car crash, heading home to us on a windswept road one night during a hurricane.

I remember my little sister's premonition that he wouldn't make it through the storm. I remember the phone ringing and my mother's anguished cries.

We had lost our breadwinner. I had lost my most important male role model.

It changed my life.

But it didn't change me – not the way the death of Robert Brown had.

When Robert Brown died, death became personal. It made me realize for the first time that some day my name would be called and I wouldn't answer.

page 126

At the funeral, we were bitter because we felt he never got a chance to live his life.

We were wrong.

The 13 years that came crashing to a close on the road that night represented Robert Brown's entire life.

Lately I've had to remember that and the "untimely" deaths of three close friends I've lost in the last few years.

Their faces keep flashing into my consciousness as I try to process the feelings the tragic death of Hank Gathers have drawn out of me.

He never got a chance to live his life, I want to say. But I know better.

The tragedy is not just that Hank Gathers died so young. It is that he didn't get to do all the things he was trying to do.

But it was the trying that defined his life. We will remember him because we saw what he was trying to do.

He wanted to get his family out of the projects. But they couldn't have loved him any more if he had.

There was a point in December when he learned that his heart did not beat with a regular rhythm. He could have decided then to quit playing basketball and try to save his life.

His decision was that the life he'd save would not be his own. Which is not to say that he couldn't have fashioned another kind of life for himself.

But at the age of 23, he was man enough to decide what he wanted his life to be and to live it that way.

It makes no more sense for us to second-guess that decision than it does to keep questioning why it happened to him.

Why is it that only the good die young?

Maybe it's because they have lived long enough to accomplish something.

Hank Gathers certainly did.

Young men in North Philly, Southern California and everywhere in between were energized by his life, which is more than will be said about most of us who have lived longer.

page 127

Some saw him on television or on the playgrounds or leading that incredible schoolboy team that won a city championship for Dobbins High School – and decided to go for it the way Hank did.

He didn't have to go all the way to show them the way to go.

They can learn from his short life just as they can from the short lives of the young men whose heart rhythms are stilled by bullets almost every day.

They prove that not just the good die young.

There is no way to know how good some of them could have been if they hadn't died so young.

We do know that a lot more lives are being saved than lost on the streets where Hank Gathers grew up.

And we know that he lived long enough to have something to do with that.

– March 13, 1990

From jail to Yale:
Actor's many roles

Charles Dutton tells the story of that night as if years of retelling have eroded all but the barest details.

"I was in a fight," he told a group of Temple students Tuesday. ``A guy tried to kill me. I killed him."

He spares us the particulars of a death scene that is replayed every night in America. The story would have been no better if the other guy had been the one who lived to tell it.

In fact, if Dutton had been the one who collapsed and died on that East Baltimore street, we wouldn't care about either man's story.

But he may never outlive that night. So he tells the story quickly, without emotion. Survivors may have regrets, but not remorse.

By now, the story of his survival on the streets of East Baltimore and in the Maryland prison system is mere background detail in one of those classic redemption tales that we never tire of.

"The difference between me and a lot of the guys who never left Greenmount Ave.," he told me before going out to address his audience ``is that I found that one thing that I was made to do."

"I'm not the only one who made it, either. I could take you to a lot of guys back home who broke out of it and became great mechanics or carpenters.

"They raise their children and take care of their wives. They don't get the respect I get because their jobs aren't in the spotlight like mine. But I respect them. I know what they came through."

page 129

It's a theme that he returns to later as he outlines his improbable odyssey for the theater majors and others in his audience.

He tells them about ``going from jail to Yale," never once making the phony and pious point that if he can make it anyone can. He's not just anyone and he doesn't pretend to be.

He gives them the details about reading Douglas Turner Ward's "Day of Absence" through the thin shards of light that filtered through the bars into his 5-by-7 cell in solitary confinement and how it opened his soul.

Then he steps into their experience with the story of his struggle to finish college as a drama major at Towson State College and his being accepted by Yale University drama school, where he graduated in the class of '84 with Angela Bassett and John Turturro.

Parts of his story must seem unreal even to him at times.

Like the time he, Denzel Washington, Wesley Snipes, Samuel L. Jackson and Morgan Freeman shared three hot dogs on a street corner in Manhattan, or when he went to South Africa and met with President Nelson Mandela.

"The first thing he asked me," Dutton said ``is `so, when is Joey [his shiftless brother on the since-canceled series "Roc"] going to get a job?'

"I didn't know who the hell he was talking about at first. But "Roc" was the No. 1 show in South Africa in 1994."

It's been a year since ``Roc" was canceled after a three-year run on Fox-TV. His voice betrays a trace of bitterness as he talks about its failure and what he thinks it says about the chance for positive portrayals of black families on TV.

"Roc" was more than a role. He agreed to do it only after negotiating assurances that he would be free to assemble the cast, have creative control and part ownership of the show.

There was no mistaking his imprint. He managed to make it funny and still deliver a message that was meaningful without being heavy-handed.

But after three years of shifting time slots and diminishing ratings, Fox pulled the plug.

page 130

"They couldn't wait to get rid of it," he said. `` . . . In the 50-year history of TV, blacks were always consigned to the buffoon zone.

"Imagine if `Married with Children' was the only image white people had of themselves on TV. They can laugh at that because at 9 o'clock, they get to run the world again. They can see themselves as doctors and lawyers again."

He seems to ignore the positive portrayals of blacks on dozens of TV shows that run after 9 o'clock and downplays the fact that Fox-TV has presented more black sitcoms than any other network.

But Dutton's disdain for the kind of black-oriented comedy that dominates TV and for a lack of honest portrayals of black life reflect more of what he learned in East Baltimore than what he's lived in West Hollywood.

He contrasts his five-year sentence for killing a black man with the eight years he got for hitting a white guard in jail.

His biting criticism of black comics like Martin Lawrence and Jimmy Walker and the cast of ``Living Single" reflects his overall world view and can only be understood in that context.

One black student asked him how a black actor can balance his need to make a living and his desire to make a statement.

"It's a good question," he said, softening.

He answered it with a story about meeting Sammy Davis Jr. on an airplane. He had always considered Davis ``an Uncle Tom."

But by the time they got to L.A. he wished he could go back and erase from his memory all the disparaging comments he had ever made about the man.

He may feel that way about Martin Lawrence and Jimmy Walker some day too. If he does, you can bet he'll be man enough to say so.

– *February 9, 1996*

page 131

William
'The Jeffersons'
Clinton

Our 'first black prez' is movin' on up – to Harlem!

You had to know Our Bill was coming home.

Where else would the man known as America's first black president seek refuge as his tormentors stoked a fire under his stew pot?

Who else would set a table for him in the presence of his enemies?

What better time to discover the wonders of Harlem than when the burdens of downtown rent get too heavy to bear?

So the only surprise yesterday as Bill Clinton stood outside his new offices on the corner of Martin Luther King Jr. and Malcolm X boulevards is what took him so long to find his way home.

That's right, home. Arkansas may be his birthplace, but his downhome homies voted for George W. Bush. Harlem went for Gore.

Back in Washington he's about as popular as double-digit inflation.

In Harlem, church ladies will serve him sweet tea from their tallest jelly jars.

In Washington, they're more likely to serve him a subpoena.

So, like Quasimodo at Notre Dame, Bill Clinton has found refuge in a place where he can ring his bell without getting busted for disturbing the peace.

He may want to hold up on the bell-ringing, though. Might be wise to check in with local leaders before he gets too loud.

page 132

I couldn't help noticing that the Rev. Al Sharpton wasn't on the welcome wagon yesterday.

Sharpton, who occupies more modest office space in the same building as Bill Clinton's penthouse suite, seemed a little cool to the homecoming.

"This could be the ultimate case of gentrification," Sharpton told reporters on Monday.

"We allow visitors as long as they know how to behave... I also want to make sure it's good news for the neighborhood."

But I wouldn't worry about it. A guy who can host high tea for Yasser Arafat and Menachem Begin will figure out how to observe the proper protocols with Big Al.

If nothing else, this move away from the $800,000-a-year suite he had hoped to rent in the Carnegie Towers puts him 10 miles closer to his suburban home and 10 miles farther from Washington.

In the Harlems of the world, there's no more coveted badge of honor than the tooth marks of your enemies.

Last they heard he was sending back the White House furniture that he and Hillary mistakenly packed along with their stuff.

The new administration was busy reversing the executive orders he issued in his last week, the Justice Department was investigating his 11th-hour pardon of millionaire tax dodger Marc Rich.

And our own Arlen Specter was pondering the possibility that he might still find a way to impeach him even though he is no longer in office. What's at stake, Specter says, is whether he deserves a presidential pension.

You don't want Republicans mad at you. They've got that dreaded pit bull overbite. Once they lock on your, leg you've got to amputate at the knee to get loose.

But in the Harlems of the world, there's no more coveted badge of honor than the tooth marks of your enemies.

page 133

Black leaders have known that for years. When Adam Clayton Powell wasn't holed up in his unforced exile on the isle of Bimini, he could always come home to Harlem.

When Clarence Thomas felt heat from unscrupulous Democrats bent on derailing his Supreme Court nomination, he reached out to the one community where forgiveness is served up in heaping portions.

This is nothing more than "a high-tech lynching," his honor said, summoning up imagery sure to evoke knowing nods in a community that always forgives its own.

So Bill is safe in the arms of the people who loved him best, the one place where they can look at a crown of thorns and see a laurel wreath.

He's a short walk from the healing power of soul food, on a street where enterprising brothers in dashikis do a bustling trade in fragrant oils and bootleg videos.

If he needs security, the Fruit of Islam will send some bowtied brothers to form a phalanx and make his forced retreat look like a victory march.

Of course, Republicans will find a way to link this move to his support of Harlem's Empowerment zones. There will be a probe, maybe even an indictment.

But even bad news ain't so bad when you're home with the people who love you.

— February 14, 2001

For tireless Mandela, there's still work to do

He says he will retire to obscurity and roam the hills of his boyhood village. But former South African President Nelson Mandela can never retire.

If he could, he would have returned to his beloved hills nine years ago. After 27 years in prison, three years in European exile and three years hiding in his homeland, he had earned the rest he dreams of.

He should have been somewhere in sweet repose, a lion in winter, warm in his shaggy coat with young lions grooming his graying mane. But they still needed him then.

So he walked out of prison and stepped into the leadership of a morally bankrupt nation.

"I place the remaining years of my life in your hands," he told an expectant throng who waited outside the prison gates for his release almost 10 years ago.

It had to be him. He was the one man with the moral authority to sell South Africa's oppressed blacks on the idea of reconciliation instead of revenge. Nelson Mandela translated his own forgiveness and forbearance into a national policy, persuaded his people that the revenge they deserved was a luxury they couldn't afford.

Repressed resentments still simmer. But the nation whose reins he relinquishes today is closer to the peace and equality he envisioned than at any time in its blood-soaked history.

So why not retire to the hills? Why shouldn't he be free to enjoy a quiet life with his new wife, Graca Machel, or to spend time with the grandchildren he fawns over every chance he gets?

Because he has never mastered the knack of resting while there is work to do.

page 135

Fifty years ago, he could have told himself that the best thing he could do for his people was to donate some money to their cause.

He was the eldest son of a respected chief, a partner in South Africa's first black-owned law firm. He could have contented himself with pro bono work for blacks who could not afford to fight the institutionalized injustice of South Africa's racist courts.

But he couldn't get comfortable in the midst of his people's agony. He wouldn't let the leaders of South Africa's apartheid state catch him in the contradiction of the ``if I made it you can too" mythology that separates the fortunate few from the masses.

He won't be able to rest now either. He will gladly step out of the spotlight so that his successor, Thabo Mbeki, will not have to rule from his immense shadow. Stepping out of harness is something else altogether.

Requests for his services started arriving in diplomatic pouches as he was cleaning out his desk. He has tentatively agreed to act as a mediator in the hostilities between Myanmar's ruling military and the leaders of Burma's pro-democracy movement.

The U.S. State Department has looked to South Africa as the symbol of democracy for southern Africa if not for the entire continent. Much of the personal diplomacy toward that end will undoubtedly fall to Mandela.

The former president has maintained his status as an international peacemaker by defying U.S. policy on Libya. The U.S. State Department cried foul when Mandela gave its highest award to Libyan leader Moammar Gadhafi last year. Later, when he traveled to Libya to confer with Gadhafi, U.S. leaders made their disagreement public.

But Mandela's intercession with Gadhafi is now seen as the key influence in Gadhafi's decision earlier this year to allow two indicted Libyan suspects to stand trial in the Netherlands for the Pan Am 103 bombing.

"I place the remaining years of my life in your hands," he pledged. It's a promise he wouldn't know how to break.

– June 16, 1999

page 136

Remember his stands,
not his marches

The first alarm was in the frantic voice of a mother desperate to reach her son with a warning.

"When he gets off duty, tell him to stay in," she said. "No telling how he's going to act when he hears that they killed King."

They killed King?! After a moment of stunned silence, I passed the word to her son and the other soldiers stationed with us at a Nike missile site in Edgmont, Pa.

We all reacted the same way.

But dazed expressions soon gave way to knowing nods. We were shocked, but not surprised.

The bullet that ripped his throat open and left Dr. Martin Luther King Jr. dead on the balcony of a seedy motel was fired by a petty thief who had stalked him for days before lining him up in the crosshairs of his gunsight that night in Memphis.

But the shot could have been fired on a hundred other nights by a dozen different assassins.

The slithering snake who hid in the bushes and killed Medgar Evers a few feet from home where his wife and children waited for him, or the craven cowards who killed four little girls in Birmingham, or the rabid racists who maimed and murdered three civil rights workers outside Meridian, Miss., would have killed King gladly.

"By 1958, the FBI had investigated 58 plots to kill him," wrote Richard Lischer, a Duke University divinity professor, in a biography called "The Preacher King."

King had been preparing his followers and family for years.

page 137

"Morning after morning, you get up and look into the faces of your children and wife not knowing whether you will get back to them because you are living under the threat of death," Lischer quotes King as saying.

He was the point man in a movement that did more to change America than any movement in this century.

But as the silent witness of a hundred martyred freedom fighters attests, we didn't all welcome the change.

King understood from the start that if he didn't get out soon, he wouldn't get out alive.

But he was obsessed by a vision that America would "rise up and live out the true meaning of its creed that all men are created equal."

That vision and an almost messianic zeal that propelled him "morning after morning" through dangers seen and unseen is what we are commemorating.

We celebrate his life on the anniversary of his death only because the 30 years since that night in Memphis have seen a new generation come of age, a generation that can't remember an America that people died to change.

This is not about conspiracy theories.

The fact that a third-rate crook who couldn't pull off a gas station stick-up managed to elude everyone from the FBI to Scotland Yard on a four-month chase through four countries is prima facie evidence that James Earl Ray was just a trigger man in a well-financed conspiracy.

But he's a minor footnote in one of the most important chapters in 20th-century American history. Tracing the source of his support is no more important now than tracing the source of the lead in the bullet that killed King.

Thirty years later, the more important questions surround the true identity of the martyr, not the assassins.

He wasn't the man they said he was. Martin Luther King Jr. was not the race-baiting rabble rouser his critics claimed, nor the passive, peace-at-all costs accommodationist of popular myth.

page 138

If he had lived to follow the course he had set by 1968, there wouldn't be a national holiday in his honor today. His shift toward broader social issues and courageous criticism of American foreign policy in Vietnam, Africa and the Caribbean were already starting to alienate much of the wide-ranging support he had enjoyed in the civil-rights struggle.

His call for a bill of rights for the disadvantaged, his harsh criticism of a black middle class that he said was too often "unmoved and untouched by the agonies and struggles" of the poor would have begun to chip away at the solid base of his support.

He would not have been silent on issues like abortion rights and welfare reform and the death penalty. Wherever he stood on those issues would have put him opposite some of the same people who linked arms with him to face police dogs and assassins' bullets.

If death threats didn't deter him, he certainly would not have sacrificed his principles for popularity.

But in the past 30 years, well-meaning admirers have turned him into an icon as revered, and as lifeless, as a sacred statue or cherished amulet. Each succeeding wreath we lay at his tomb smothers his fire under another layer of flowery speeches.

His "I Have a Dream" speech is recited by children the way James Weldon Johnson's "The Creation" was when I was a child. With every recitation he becomes more dreamlike, less real.

But they don't shoot dreamers; they let them sleep.

King was a target because he forced the nation to face the inconsistencies between its egalitarian rhetoric and discriminatory reality.

"So we have come to cash this check," King said in a part of the "dream" speech that seldom gets quoted. "A check that will give us on demand the riches of freedom and the security of justice."

He didn't come with his hat in his hand, either.

"We know from painful experience that freedom is never given voluntarily by the oppressor," he said in a sermon. "It has to be demanded by the oppressed."

page 139

It's a philosophy that we are more likely to ascribe to Malcolm X, a King contemporary who is generally thought to have been much more confrontational than King. But, in reality, it was King who confronted the establishment while Malcolm's message was mostly family business.

It was King and not Malcolm who was branded in an internal FBI memo in August 1963 as "the most dangerous Negro of the future in this nation." A month later, FBI head J. Edgar Hoover got Attorney General Robert Kennedy to sign an order allowing him to wiretap King's home and offices in Atlanta and New York.

Still, armchair historians tend to equate the differences between Martin and Malcolm with the philosophical gulf that separated Booker T. Washington and Dr. W.E.B. Du Bois.

Du Bois was the black nationalist intellectual who linked the deprivations of American blacks with the sufferings of colonized people all over the world.

Washington was an accommodationist who urged blacks to forget about being accorded equality and learn to live comfortably as second-class citizens.

But King called Washington's approach "pressureless persuasion" and "passive acceptance".

"He was honored and heralded everywhere as a responsible leader," King once wrote of Washington. "I always get a little disturbed when I'm referred to as a responsible leader.

"It may mean that you are concerned with saying what the white power structure wants to hear."

Malcolm and King came to a meeting of the minds just before Malcolm was murdered. Before that, they were separated more by religion and tactics than by philosophy. In his most stinging indictment, Malcolm called King "the reverend doctor chicken wing" and accused him of preaching pie in the sky.

But it was far from truth.

"It's all right to talk about streets flowing with milk and honey over yonder," King counseled in a March 3,1963, sermon at Ebenezer Baptist Church in Atlanta. "But let's get some food to eat for people down here in Asia and Africa and South America and in our own nation."

"Racism and its perennial ally, economic exploitation, provide the key to understanding most of the international complications of this generation," he said in a 1964 speech. "The powerful nations of the world are incapable of taking a moral position against apartheid in South Africa."

He was never more eloquent in making that link between the "perennial allies" than in his scathing criticism of America's conduct in Vietnam.

"So we have been repeatedly faced with the cruel irony of watching Negro and white boys on TV screens as they kill and die together," he said in a 1964 interview in Redbook magazine.

"We watch them in brutal solidarity burning the huts of a poor village. But we realize that they would never live on the same block together in Detroit. I could not be silent in the face of such cruel manipulation of the poor."

I don't believe he could have been silent in the face of today's "cruel irony" either. Thirty years after his death, the disparities and inequities he fought and died to reverse are in some ways more pronounced than they were then.

"The Millennium Breach," a massive study that the Milton S. Eisenhower Foundation released last month, details the growing gap between the rich and poor in America:

• "America's neighborhoods and schools are resegregating," the report concludes. Two-thirds of minority students now attend predominantly minority schools where two-thirds of the pupils score below basic proficiency levels in national tests.

• Just in the 1980s alone, child poverty increased by more than 20 percent, making America's child poverty rate four times the average of Western European countries.

• Between 1977 and 1988, the incomes of the richest 1 percent in America increased by 120 percent, while the incomes of the poorest fifth decreased by 10 percent. The top 1 percent of Americans has more wealth than the bottom 90 percent.

page 141

King had set a course to confront the very policies and lack of policies that have resulted in these disparities. He had begun to organize coalitions of poor blacks, Appalachian whites, Hispanics and native Americans into voting blocs.

In his book, "Where Do We Go from Here?" an increasingly radical King was already starting to focus on the failure of urban school systems and what he saw as their growing tendency to scapegoat parents and pupils.

"Whatever pathology may exist in Negro families is far exceeded by the social pathology in the school system that refuses to accept a responsibility," he wrote. "The job of the schools is to teach so well that family background is no longer an issue."

King was a consistent critic of what he called "sham" welfare programs that offered handouts, but no hope. He was suspicious of training programs that had no job guarantees attached.

"Training," King wrote, "becomes a way of avoiding the issue of employment."

Where he would have gone from Memphis and how many of us would have marched with him is an open question. But the lesson of the 30 years since his death is that we can't afford to march in place.

– April 2, 1998

Beckwith verdict won't change much in Delta

The guy at the Citgo in Yazoo City said I couldn't miss it if I stayed on I-49. He was wrong.

Tchula is easy to miss.

You can miss ItaBena, Nitta Yuma and Panther Burn the same way.

And if you're not careful, you might blow right by Belzoni and Winona and Satartia, too.

There aren't too many must-see stops along I-49 in the Mississippi Delta.

Tchula is not one of them.

The road into the south side of town is lined by leaning shacks, rusting trailers and the commercial holdings of Mr. McKinley Young.

McKinley Young's success story is the kind you have to read between the lines.

He owns the South Side Cafe, a rundown beer joint across the street and a narrow counter with a few dozen small bottles that he calls his package store.

Except for the new Buick parked behind the South Side cafe, his properties are not distinguished by any obvious trappings of success.

The cafe is a cinderblock box with a few mismatched tables and chairs.

The beer joint is a room with a juke box, a beer cooler and a coin operated pool table.

It seats about 10 but that's more than enough because most of his patrons do their drinking standing up in a dusty lot outside.

page 143

"Everything you see here is mine," Young told me.

"I don't owe nobody nothing – not even the bank. And if I do go to the bank I don't go begging."

You don't have to beg when you have seven hundred acres of rich Delta land producing $300 per acre with every cotton crop.

Young could be the Tchula Chamber of Commerce poster boy.

He's living proof that times have changed in the Delta since Medgar Evers died trying 31 years ago.

But there hasn't been 30 years worth of change in Tchula. And what change there has been wasn't always for the better.

"That's all some of them want to do is smoke that stuff," Young said.

Four blocks away, a group of young men stood on a corner selling drugs.

"But a black man can make it in Mississippi today. Medgar Evers and Dr. King died so we could make it better."

His patrons in and around the beer joint don't share his view of Mississippi as a land of opportunity. Most of them are under 30 and out of work.

"There's no place to work in the winter if you wanted to," said a young man named Marshall Tate.

"We're supposed to be so happy 'cause blacks and whites can work together now. But Mississippi Chemical has laid off so many now, the white ones is out of work, too."

Young, 74, does have this in common with the restless black youths who buy his beer.

They're all rooting for Byron De La Beckwith to go to jail for the rest of his life.

They want it for different reasons. Young seems to want to believe things are different in the Delta, that the justice system works for black people now.

The younger ones across the street could care less about history. Racism is still a current event for them.

They have never really been afraid of night riders or lynch mobs.

And no matter what happens to Beckwith, they still won't believe the justice system works for them.

page 144

They talk about revenge in general terms.

"It ain't gonna change nothing," said Garrett Jackson. "I just think they ought to kill him or let his old ass rot in jail."

"Anytime you just kill a man and go bragging about it, you ought to be dead."

So young and old will be in accord for a change. They'll be listening to the radio, waiting for the verdict.

Beckwith's jury is expected to begin deliberating today in the Hinds County Court House in Jackson.

His fate is in their hands, but only his. It's not gonna change much in the Mississippi Delta either way.

– February 4, 1994

In the heat of battle, Thomas recalls roots

Let me open today's column with a word of welcome for my brother Clarence Thomas who had been away on business until this weekend.

Welcome home, bro.

He was off advancing his career in the secret places of the most high when the colorblind society he ran with suddenly regained its sight.

At least that's the way it was, to hear him tell it.

A "high-tech lynching for uppity blacks who in any way deign to think for themselves, to do for themselves, to have different ideas," is the way Judge Thomas described the ugly turn his confirmation charade took last week.

And it does have a certain resonance in the black community. It certainly did with me, anyway.

Because after weeks of watching him be whatever he had to be, say whatever he had to say to get in and fit in with the right crowd, it was great to see him move his mouth without some Republican's hand up his back.

It gave television's longest-running quiz show, "To Tell The Truth," just the right jolt when the real Clarence Thomas stood up to his inquisitors and spewed righteous indignation through clenched teeth and flaring nostrils.

I guess that's what we saw.

After watching into the wee hours of yesterday morning until my eyes were glassy and my head ached from data overload, I'm still not sure who was telling the truth.

To hear him and his band of loyalists tell it, a bunch of liberal Democrats lobbed a stink bomb at his otherwise unblemished and undistinguished judicial record.

page 146

He seems to believe they got together and produced this willing dupe in an understated dress to make out like Thomas had said something nasty to her while she worked as his special assistant.

His fellow Yale Law alum, Anita Hill, held America spellbound with her sordid testimony about how Thomas allegedly sexually harassed her while she worked closely with him in two federal agencies.

Just how closely is open to speculation. So are his movie viewing habits, and even the proportions of what he's packing in his pants, thanks to the hours of repeated references to things best left unsaid.

But they weren't left unsaid, Thomas says, because he is black. If he were white, we're left to conclude, the boys in the back room would have cleaned this mess up before it stained our national psyche.

So, I wasn't sure if he was so angry because they treated him differently or because the whole thing was a lie conjured up by a conspiracy of powerful white folks out to block a brother's rise to the top.

Because it didn't sound like a lie to me – at least not one conjured up by white folks.

Clarence Thomas certainly has white enemies, but the world's most powerful white folks, people who don't have much to do with other blacks, are on his side, including George Bush.

And his list of supporters includes such luminaries as Orrin the Hack Hatch and Sen. Strom Thurmond, the man listed in the Guinness Book of Records as having the longest anti-civil rights filibuster in U.S. history (24 hours and 19 minutes from Aug. 28-29, 1957, for you history buffs).

It's enough to recall a lesson his granddaddy must have taught him back in Pinpoint, Ga.: "People judge you by the company you keep."

Furthermore, Anita Hill got trashed as much by Thomas' supporters as he did by her alleged co-conspirators. She stood her ground in a calm and dispassionate way as her aged parents sat by listening to their youngest of 13 children give testimony that may do more harm to her future than it will to the man she has accused.

page 147

For the next two days she was savaged by people who portrayed her as an ambitious, unscrupulous, vindictive woman who conspired to topple a man who had done nothing but give his best for her.

I can't buy that one. The only thing harder to figure than why she maintained what she called "a cordial relationship" with her alleged tormentor is what is in this for her.

She and Thomas were cut from the same cloth politically. She supported the nomination of Robert Bork, worked for conservative causes. They certainly were not political enemies.

And the business about her fantasizing the whole thing is just a lame fallback position offered up by Republican senators who want to raise the possibility that everybody is telling the truth.

Somebody is lying. And we'll probably never know who it is.

The only sure thing out of this is that 25 million black folks, including two whose accomplishments should be filling us with pride, are being dragged through the mud.

It's enough to make you retch.

There's not a whole lot to salvage out of this one. The one thing we can do is to welcome Clarence Thomas home.

We can forget the way his conservative allies used the same bootstraps he pulled himself up by to put down a growing "underclass" they claim are too shiftless and lazy and dependent on government handouts to accomplish what he has.

We can only hope that if he does get to the Supreme Court, he'll remember where he came from – and who he ran back to when he got into trouble that time.

– *October 15, 1991*

Recognition and privacy
Somehow, Jesse must provide both for this child

The most poignant passage in Marshall Frady's meticulously researched biography of Jesse Jackson shows Jackson standing outside his father's house.

Noah Robinson Sr. had moved his family to a big house in a better part of Greenville, S.C., across town from the little shack where his "outside" son Jesse Jackson was born.

Robinson, a prosperous cotton buyer, had never acknowledged this boy that many in Greenville's close-knit black community knew to be his son.

The outside son hoped to catch a glimpse of his father that night and perhaps to be seen and acknowledged by him and his siblings. It didn't happen.

Later, Jackson's athletic prowess and his widely known status as an honor student earned him his father's begrudging acknowledgement. But that only fueled his drive for legitimacy.

Frady, in the acclaimed biography "Jesse," theorizes that the pain of that rejection and estrangement from his natural father was the crucible that formed the Jesse Jackson we know today.

The "anonymous man outside" who would not accept that his boundaries were formed by the circumstances of his birth recast himself in heroic proportions.

Nice theory. It may even be true.

But it's not what Jackson remembered when he found himself in the role of his late father two years ago.

He remembered the hurt of being rejected by a father everyone looked up to as if it was he and not the father who had failed his family.

page 149

So he and Karin Stanford, the mother of his 20-month old daughter, made a pact. She would move back to California with their child. He would provide a comfortable living for her as he had for his children with his wife, Jackie.

And he would love the child.

"As her mother does," Jackson said in a written statement, "I love this child very much."

That may not absolve him for infidelity or mend the tattered fabric of a family that must feel betrayed as he did that night when he stood outside his father's house.

But his love child will at least be loved and provided for. And acknowledged.

"I was born of these circumstances and I know the importance of growing up in a nurturing, supportive and protective environment," he said in his statement.

"So, I am determined to give my daughter and her mother the privacy they both deserve."

That last part may be a tall order.

The same media that Jackson has been able to manipulate and maneuver in for years will be loath to grant them that privacy.

The disclosures three years ago that Julius Erving is the father of tennis pro Alexandra Stevenson set off a feeding frenzy by media who hounded her for the next few weeks until the novelty wore off.

Jackson and his wife managed to shield their children from most of the media glare as they were growing up.

Jackson and Karin Stanford must at least try to do the same for this new child.

But stories like this don't just slip out. They get pushed. For all its legendary aggression, reporters rarely dig up this much detail without being led to it.

Almost nothing about Jesse Jackson can remain private for very long.

His decision to shun the spotlight for a while as he tries to reconcile with his family may protect all of them for a time.

But my hope for him and us is that this will not end his career. Millions of Americans, including 15 million voters, from every race and region have been moved by his message.

page 150

He has huddled with heads of state, freed hostages, affected summit level negotiations and settled bitter disputes.

It's still Jesse.

Tomorrow, he will watch from the sidelines as Bill Clinton leaves office.

Clinton will leave with the highest approval rating ever for a departing president.

But Clinton also earned the lowest rating for personal integrity and honesty of any president in recorded history.

Jesse Jackson may suffer a similar fate. His enemies will gloat as his supporters suffer with him. It goes with the territory.

But the one thing he will never be again is the anonymous man outside.

– January 19, 2001

Grieving daughter sucked into plot?

She was there, watched her father take the stage – tall, proud. She heard him speak, heard the crowd's cheers confirm what every little girl knows about her father, that he was the most important man on earth.

She must have heard the men shouting from one side of the Audubon Ballroom stage in New York in what she now knows was a trick to distract his bodyguards. The rest must be a blur.

Betty Shabazz, who was pregnant at the time, has said she forced her four young daughters to the floor when the first shot rang out. They may not have seen the gunmen advance on him and fire the fatal shots.

But the sound of those shots, the screams, the anguish, the chaos, may ring in Qubilah Shabazz's ears forever. She set up her life outside the spotlight, lived quietly sometimes overseas.

There could be no refuge from the repeated reminders of his life and death, though. She named her own son Malcolm and lived with the memory.

But 30 years later, our government tells us, she conspired with a government informant in a plot to kill the man she believed plotted to kill her father.

We may never know who killed Malcolm. They arrested some gunmen, sent them to jail. They may have fired the shots.

But who issued the orders? Who dispatched the gunmen?

page 152

Some believe the same government that went after his daughter last week was a behind-the-scenes player in the plot to kill Malcolm. Betty Shabazz has always said Minister Louis Farrakhan was one of the men behind the plot.

And now we can only pray that her daughter Qubilah did not target Farrakhan for death in some misguided plot that could only perpetuate a tragic legacy of violence.

If she did, if her sorrow and anger have fermented for 30 years into some intoxicating vision of herself as the chosen vehicle to bring her father's killer to justice, at least that's a motivation we can understand.

But what was our government doing in this? If the Justice Department was aware of this plot, why didn't it step in and stop it sooner?

Instead we're left to ponder the possibility that our government egged her on, led her further and further into this insane scheme until they had her trapped in a mess they helped to make.

And that's the part that involves us all. This is not some black thang that you wouldn't understand. None of us understand it, either.

But someone owes us all an explanation. If Qubilah Shabazz is involved, she should be punished.

But there's another co-conspirator here and it's us – or people acting on our behalf.

So somebody explain to me how my national interests have been furthered by this scheme to draw this troubled young woman in over her head? How have we benefited from a plot to trap a woman with no history of violence or criminality?

Radio stations here in L.A. are reporting that a government videotape shows her expressing strong reservations about this plot she supposedly hatched.

If that's so, why didn't someone step in then?

Even more troubling is the government's use of a mole such as Michael Fitzpatrick. Fitzpatrick went to high school with Qubilah Shabazz at New York's exclusive United Nations International School.

By then, he was already rumored to be a member of the Irish Republican Army. He is said to have been a member of the militant Jewish Defense League while still in his teens.

page 153

FBI agents used him as an informant against the JDL after pegging him as one of the men who bombed a bookstore in New York.

Since then, every time this rodent raises his head it raises a question about government tactics. Several of his targets claim Fitzpatrick was the guiding force behind the plots they went to jail for.

According to a report in the New York Times this week, Fitzpatrick continued to dabble in anarchist causes and inform on his co-conspirators even after leaving the government's witness protection program in Minneapolis.

He was also arrested on cocaine possession charges 14 months ago, opening a rift with his government sponsors that he may have tried to repair by entrapping Qubilah Shabazz.

Maybe we can understand why the government runs its witness protection program as a kind of Club Med for criminals. I can even understand why they use little slugs such as Fitzpatrick to troll for bigger prey.

But when we turn these vermin loose on otherwise law-abiding citizens, we'd better be sure we're not creating crimes or furthering them through schemes the government conspires in.

– *January 19, 1995*

page 154

Betty has never been a victim

She had only a small supporting role in this historic scene. So Betty Shabazz delivered her line quickly then quietly faded into the background.

"I'm Betty Shabazz," she said softly, "or Mrs. Malcolm X."

Winnie Mandela, who had been seated a few feet away on the podium, stood and grabbed her.

"I could stand here and cry for hours," Betty Shabazz said a few minutes later when they finally released each other from their tearful embrace.

Instead, she handed Winnie Mandela a bouquet of flowers and quietly backed out of the spotlight.

This was at the corner of Martin Luther King and Adam Clayton Powell boulevards in a place called African Square near the center of the village of Harlem. It was June 1990 and Winnie Mandela was in New York with Nelson Mandela, who had recently returned to her and the world after 27 years in prison.

This meeting of women who had lost their men to the struggle was supposed to be a sidelight, just one brief stop in the world tour that provided Nelson Mandela with the means to set up South Africa's first democratic government. Betty Shabazz politely declined to be interviewed afterwards, opting not to draw attention away from Winnie Mandela.

But what I remember most from that day was something Betty Shabazz didn't say: She didn't say she was the widow of Malcolm X.

page 155

She has always impressed me as a woman who would sooner be scorned than pitied. She worked hard to remold herself into anything but an object of sympathy.

Betty Shabazz , pregnant with twins, and her four daughters were witnesses the day Malcolm fell in a hail of assassins' bullets in New York's Audubon Ballroom. But she had been a "widow" long before that, raising their children virtually alone as Malcolm's ministry seemed to send him everywhere but home.

Somehow, with six small children, she managed to put herself through school, earning a Ph.D. Dr. Betty Shabazz forged a career at Medgar Evers College. She worked hard and raised her babies and refused to robe herself in the cloak of victimization. Now, as she struggles to survive the flames that threaten to consume the life she fashioned for herself, she will want our prayers but not our pity.

And I believe she will want our prayers for her 12-year-old grandson, Malcolm, who stands accused of setting a fire that could destroy his future as well as hers.

The widely circulated story that he doused her apartment in gasoline, then waited for his grandmother to come home before igniting it, may or may not be true. If he did it, we don't know why. It can't be as simple as the published speculation that he hated living with his grandmother.

It is the latest bizarre plot twist in the longest-running family tragedy since the trials of Job. Despite all her exertions and her incredible strength, she has not been able to shield her family from the consequences of its fate.

She raised her daughters in the suburbs, sent them to the best schools. But it was at the prestigious United Nations School where her daughter Qubilah met Michael Fitzpatrick, a paid FBI informant who later capitalized on her obsession to avenge her father's death.

Betty Shabazz had always believed that Minister Louis Farrakhan played an active role in her husband's murder. She said so in public.

There has never been any evidence that Minister Farrakhan played an active role, although he acknowledges that some of his rhetoric may have inadvertently helped create the atmosphere the assassination plot was hatched in.

page 156

Qubilah, too, blamed her father's death on Farrakhan and eventually came to believe her mother's life was in danger. She and Fitzpatrick allegedly plotted to assassinate Farrakhan. For drawing her further into this plot, the FBI paid Fitzpatrick about $45,000 – the 1995 equivalent of 30 pieces of silver.

Betty Shabazz did everything a mother could to save her child. And in what must have been a bitter irony, she ultimately accepted the help of Farrakhan, who threatened to expose Qubilah's prosecution for the sordid mess it was.

I was outside the federal courthouse in Minneapolis the day Betty Shabazz came to collect her daughter. Qubilah had been absolved in a deal, the government getting to say she was guilty without punishing her or exposing its own part in the slimy plot with Fitzpatrick.

Betty and Qubilah Shabazz, flanked by attorney Percy Sutton and the now-deceased cause counselor William Kunstler, praised Farrakhan in an impromptu press conference.

"I want to express my appreciation and surprise to him for his kind words, his patience and his generosity," Betty Shabazz said.

Those may have been her true feelings. But what was also true is that her daughter's life was more important at that point than her husband's death.

The deal that freed Qubilah Shabazz required that she spend the next few months in psychiatric treatment in San Antonio. Her son Malcolm went to live with his grandmother.

It would be a tragic irony if it turns out that the deal that saved her daughter spawned the suffering Betty Shabazz now endures.

But she's not just another victim for us to pity. And I'd bet anything that even through her pain, her first thought is of her family.

– June 3, 1997

page 157

Sammy was always 'on'
... And he probably gave too much of himself

They sealed no mysteries into the crypt with Sammy Davis Jr.'s corpse.

The complexities of his life, even the agonizing details of his death, were played out in full view of the audience whose approval he sought so desperately. The life of Sammy Davis Jr. was performed, as much as it was lived.

There were no mysteries.

But there were paradoxes. He was an enigma, sometimes even to himself.

We know this because he told us so. Often.

He told us about his identity crises, recurrent self-image problems, his battles with drink, drugs and Satanism.

"I Gotta Be Me," he kept telling us - as if he really knew who that was.

Not that he wasn't real. His life was as real as any staged event could ever be.

But you can't be "on" every day without blurring the distinction between role and reality.

He clung tenaciously – if unsuccessfully – to his tenuous ties with "everyday" reality. He tells us in his last book "Why Me?" that he needed to be a star.

But he also needed to be one of the boys. It's part of the paradox that keeps him just out of the reach of our understanding.

He lived in and for the spotlight. And if it followed him into what should have been his private life, he seemed to prefer that to the darkness of anonymity.

page 158

We may never be able to discern the truth of his life. But we knew most of the facts.

Sometimes we knew too much for his own good.

We certainly got too close a look at the final flickers of his failing light.

Did we need to know he had shriveled down to 60 pounds or that he reportedly was curled in a fetal position on his deathbed?

Weren't there too many shots of old friends emerging from his Beverly Hills home, still shaken from having seen him that way?

Photographers and reporters joined morbid curiosity seekers in a death watch outside his home.

Did they need to report the resonance of the death rattle in his dying breath?

Planeloads of his "closest" friends winged in. School kids hustled maps to his home to people who felt entitled to be there at the end.

And what should have been a poignant and private moment with intimate loved ones became a crowded closing scene.

But what else would you expect?

In death, as he had been in life, he was a piece public property.

This is not a criticism of his friends and family – and certainly not of Mr. Davis.

It would be worse than hypocritical for me to come down on a guy who freely gave what I spend much of my time trying to extract from other public people.

But the way he sought public approval – and the price he paid for the resulting scrutiny – made you know why others shun the spotlight.

Everything about him, from the jewels at his fingers to his equally gaudy talent, screamed "Look at me, look at me."

To call him a "gifted" entertainer denies him his due. No one was ever born with the talent to do all the things he did well.

He was a remarkable singer as much for his expressiveness and ability to "sell" a song as for the quality of his voice.

page 159

Songs such as "Candy Man," "I Gotta Be Me," "Who Can I Turn To?" got to be his songs, distinguished by his interpretations as much as by their composition.

But his singing improved over the years through sheer hard work. He worked hard enough at dancing to make that look easy too.

He was a consummate actor and an evocative mimic; he played drums well enough to drive a jazz band; and handled six-shooters better than most cowboy stars.

Those skills developed out of an obsession to be the world's best entertainer. And he may have been.

But he probably gave too much of himself, exposed too many dark corners of his life to the amateur analysis of the armchair psychologist in all of us.

What he got in return was a kind of begrudging admiration, tinged with the contempt that familiarity sometimes breeds.

It's the risk you run when you allow people to take their focus from themselves and put it on you.

But that's what entertainers do. And Sammy Davis Jr. may have been the best who ever did it.

– *May 22, 1990*

Acknowledgments

This is where I get into trouble. The toughest thing about acknowledgments for me is knowing where to end the list.

Knowing where to start is easy. Zack Stalberg is editor-in-chief of the Philadelphia Daily News and enabler-in-chief to me. There would be nothing to acknowledge without him.

To the aptly renowned Signe Wilkinson, a dear friend and respected colleague whose work graces these pages. Rob King whose work on the cover was the first thing you saw when you picked up this book.

To Wayne Faircloth, whose technical assistance smoothed a rough passage for me. The news research department at the Daily News, especially Ed Voves.

To Frank Burgos, editor of the Daily News opinion pages who pretended not to notice that I was working my project on his time.

To Carol Towarnicky, Sandy Shea, Don Harrison, Michael Schefer, Mark Alan Hughes, members of our editorial board who have sometimes agreed with me and, more importantly, disagreed in ways that caused me to hone or abandon some of my arguments.

Richard Aregood, now editorial page editor at the Newark Star-Ledger is simply the best editorial writer I've ever read or met. As my first opinion editor at the Daily News, his understated guidance helped me to develop my own voice when all I really wanted was to sound like him.

page 161

A special thanks to DeWayne Wickham, an extraordinary columnist whose work with the Trotter Group and the Institute of Advanced Journalism at Delaware State University have provided me with valuable professional enrichment experiences.

To the trustee board at the Tabernacle Baptist Church in Burlington, N.J., who unwittingly provided some of the content herein, especially my trustee chairman Eddie Campbell whose french fried chitterlings are a cross-cultural culinary treat.

To Ursala and the guys at Three-Star barber shop, most especially Fred Somerset who, for the past 10 years has been asking me when I was going to write a book.

You made it seem inevitable. I guess you were right.

I wish there were a way to personally thank each of the people whose words or deeds have turned up in these pages. Many of them (my family included) would just as soon have stayed out of my columns and this book if I had given them a choice. So, I didn't.

To my beautiful daughter Cheryl Arnold, her husband Capt. Aric Arnold and their daughters Ashley and Aaliyah, whose private lives have become public in these pages.

And, finally, to my savior Jesus Christ who gave Cheryl and Aric a place to land when their plane fell from the sky.

He did the same for me 13 years ago when my life was in free fall. This record would not be complete if I did not acknowledge him.

page 162